Praise for
Step Out, Step Up, Step Forward

"When you step into your true self—not who society says you are, but your true, authentic self—your whole life begins to turn around. Lori Dixon shows you how to walk the path to your own authenticity, with kindness and support. An insightful book for women seeking personal expansion."

—Sara Wiseman, author of
Messages from the Divine: Wisdom for the Seeker's Soul
www.sarawiseman.com

"Lori masterfully weaves her incredible and inspiring story with layered and important wisdom to create a book that not only entertains but becomes a powerful coaching session (or five!) for you on its own. If you are looking for more clarity, more direction, more motivation and more forward movement, this is your book."

—Joanna Lindenbaum,
author, master coach, and master facilitator
www.joannalindenbaum.com

"If you're being called to get clear on your purpose or take it to the next level, this is THE book for you. It's never too late to align to your soul's purpose and share it with the world as you'll learn from this enlightening book!"

—Jennifer Longmore,
founder of Akashic Record Training
www.souljourneys.ca

"I am impressed by Lori's commitment to rising above perceptions especially those around health and happiness. Lori continues to break through inner glass ceilings and therefore emerges to new levels of self-healing and expression."

—Dr. Ellie Drake,
founder of BraveHeart Women International

"Lori Dixon's book, *Step Out, Step Up, Step Forward: How to Walk in Your Purpose*, is set to launch soon and I can't contain my excitement. Finally, finally, finally, everyone everywhere can witness this powerhouse as she teaches us to understand our purpose and own it every step of the way! I've witnessed her magic firsthand, and there's not a day that goes by that I am not grateful for this pure light in my life. I ask you all to take a moment, buckle up, and get ready for one wild ride as Lori teaches you *How to Walk in Your Purpose*. Enjoy your life-changing journey. xo"

—David D'Orso, creative producer,
Real Housewives of Dallas Season 2

STEP OUT
STEP UP
step forward

ALSO BY LORI L. DIXON

*Step Out, Step Up, Step Forward:
Reflective Companion Journal*

Art the Easel: Creative Expression for Young Children

Co-Editor (with Janet C. Bernstein)
Every Heart Has a Story (Every Heart Project)

Anthology
Behind Her Brand Entrepreneur Edition Vol 5

STEP OUT STEP UP
step forward

How to Walk in Your Purpose

LORI L. DIXON

Copyright © 2018 by Lori L. Dixon

All rights reserved. No part of the book may be reproduced in any form or by any electronic or mechanical means, including information storage and retrieval systems, without permission in writing from the publisher, except by a reviewer who may quote brief passages in a review.

LLD Legacy Publishing
3959 Van Dyke Road, Suite 265
Lutz, FL 33558
www.WalkWithLori.com

This is a work of nonfiction. Nonetheless, some of the names and personal characteristics of the individual's involved have been changed in order to disguise their identities. Any resulting resemblance to persons living or dead is entirely coincidental and unintentional. Some individuals have given their permission to have their name and their personal story shared.

Cover design by Trey Stewart

ISBN: 1-948235-59-5
ISBN-13: 978-1-948235-59-4

*To those in my life who have supported and walked with me
in my journey to Step OUT, Step UP, Step Forward, and even leap
with vision...*

*To Art, my loving partner and soulmate...
I could not have walked this journey without you
holding my hand and giving me the hope that each
step was stronger than the one before.
You have never left my side, even when I
stumbled. As we explore life together,
I pray our steps be longer and braver.*

*To God, my soul-provider in each step I take.
May my steps be blessed and bring honor to others.*

To the mentors in my life...

*Dr. Kathryn Cramer, you bring me the wisdom of Asset-Based
Thinking and life strategies. I treasure the moments we
shared together. Please know you are missed and loved.*

*Dana West, my dear friend and constant supporter in the steps I've
taken in my life. You were there when I fell down and you
picked me up. You were there when I walked swiftly and
you celebrated. Thank you, dear one!*

*Dr. Ellie Drake, thank you for bringing me the returned feeling of
sisterhood to steer my steps into working and supporting the walk of
women. You continue to bring love and knowledge to my life and I
honor your new steps forward as the continued sage in my life.*

CONTENTS

Introduction	1
Chapter 1 *The Essential Questions of Life*	5
Chapter 2 *The Importance in Our Steps*	21
Chapter 3 *Step OUT: The Comfort Zone*	35
Chapter 4 *Step UP: Walking One Step at a Time*	75
Chapter 5 *Step Forward: The Opportunity View*	111
Chapter 6 *Envision Leaping*	141
Chapter 7 *Closing*	171

introduction

"Always remember...You are braver than you believe, stronger than you seem, and smarter than you think."
—Christopher Robin

Life is full of the steps we take, the memories we make, and the breaths we take. For me, the realization started with a glance down at the floor as I noticed the turquoise pumps with the most elegant four-inch heels. How did I get here? Life seems so different now, witnessing the beauty each day brings and the brilliant life we have the blessing of experiencing.

You see, I am a spiritual visionary and soul-based practitioner who has the opportunity to work with the most amazing women, every day, including two very special ones on *The Real Housewives of Dallas*. Appearing on RHOD Season 2 was surreal. Doing what I love every day—coaching, teaching, and being able to reach women in a greater way—is an unbelievable opportunity.

How can I understand the challenges in the lives of women I am blessed to work with each day? I am transported back to the moments I spent desperately looking for help and support myself when I asked, "What will my own story be about? What will others see in my life? What will they remember about me?" My focus is now one of empowerment and strength in knowing

I have walked so many steps of my own in difficulty, transition, and even pain and loss. Why? I want my story to be about courage, victory, and most of all, love.

There was a time when my days were spent curled up in pain on a couch, under a big thermal blanket, wearing flannel pajamas and dingy grey knit slippers lined with fleece. When I would try to get up, the severe inflammation and neurological pain my body was enduring was overwhelming. My body was failing me. I prayed that one day I could walk without losing my breath and without the constant reminder of how badly I was feeling. The difference came when I began believing it would happen.

My focus of wholeness in mind, body, and spirit perpetuated a need for answers. Sharing those "ah-ha's" with others is part of my calling and my passion so you, too, may experience healing.

Is this a book about chronic illness? Not at all. It is about how we are each given the journey to focus, learn lessons, and overcome challenges throughout life. Some of our paths appear full of pebbles where we may wobble on our "heels," while others are dips that may cause us to lose our balance. Others are boulders and detours we shift our attention to, as we wind our way around. Your journey is yours. You may struggle and fall, but you get back up with fresh insights and a stronger ability to be the "YOU" you were meant to be. Yes, my journey from the days of wearing grungy slippers to now my turquoise pumps feels like only a dream. Whatever path you are "walking" is your own "fit" and "size." Cinderella didn't start out in a glass slipper. She began in simple shoes of honor and service. We must be willing to learn from others, listen to the voice within, and expand our desire for something bigger in life.

This story is about all of us women, who live each day asking how to direct our paths with influence and impact. It is about YOU! After today, you will no longer be the same person. You will see a day miraculously envisioned through your own growth, beauty, and transformation. You are on a journey of becoming a new and beautiful version of yourself.

I share this book with women in mind, and I know the men who support and believe in us will hopefully read it and be encouraged. I pray you, the men we love, the men we treasure, the men we strive to understand and learn lessons from, will embrace our steps along the way. Thank you for being there for us and with us. We do honor and respect you in our walk.

I will share my own story of transformation, along with many of the insights and lessons my clients, colleagues, friends, and family have taught me in our conversations and interactions. In many ways, I know my path has been designed. God has a greater purpose for the journeys we are all on. As we take detours and intersect with each other, we are guided in some way to be present for someone else. In their own time, the gifts He has bestowed on us will be our magnificent treasures and most beneficial lessons, as we use them for a brighter future.

My mission continues to empower women just like you who are searching to embrace their authentic selves, to re-envision their lives, and to walk their journeys with strong intention. This allows you the ability to heal from the past, live and love in the present, and create true paths of purpose for the future. It is for this reason I share these stories, insights, tools, and strategies of my own journey and those of my clients, including two very special "housewives," Stephanie Hollman and Cary Deuber.

If your life is a story, what would it be about? Would it be about pain or purpose, tragedy or triumph, loss or love? We each have a choice in the story we tell.

Why are you choosing to read this book at this time in your life? Maybe you have been searching for answers or experiencing your own awakening to something bigger for your life, like stepping out into your own purpose aligned with your thinking. Maybe you know me, you've connected with me, and want to hear my story. Or maybe you saw me on *The Real Housewives of Dallas* as Stephanie Hollman's visionary coach and want to know how that connection and experience happened.

No matter HOW you came to hold this book in your hands, you were meant to, for no other reason but YOU and your story. Right now is the greatest and most important time in YOUR life. Embrace your moment and accept the challenge to…Step OUT, Step UP, Step FORWARD and walk with purpose in your life.

As Lao Tzu expresses so eloquently, "The journey of a thousand miles begins with one step." It is this thought that pushed me to step out, step up, and step forward as I walked further into my life and created more opportunities for me to support others along the way.

Walk with me, won't you?

Lori

chapter one
The Essential Questions of Life

One of my favorite games over the years has been Essential Questions. Instead of introducing yourself as a speaker, facilitator, or leader, you allow others to ask questions they want to know about you. Did I tell you that is only part ONE of the game?

The second part is for you to answer the questions for yourself. Space will be provided for you to answer them. You can share your thoughts on our Facebook page and be able to read what others shared too. I hope you enjoy the interaction.

These questions are based on topics I have been asked from friends, clients, colleagues, and others. Each question has been shared to create a foundation for the chapters that follow. Reflect on each question. Prepare yourself to learn more as you delve into the stories, strategies, and insights in the chapters that follow.

Step OUT, Step UP, and Step Forward!

Who am I?

Have you ever woken up and looked in the mirror and said, "Oh, my! Who IS that woman?" I sure have and probably more than once. I tend to ask, "Where did THAT new wrinkle come from?" Or even, "Did you go out late last night and I didn't know about it?" How about you? What do you say to yourself? "Oh my gosh, what happened?" "You have another gray hair, you old lady!" "Why can't you get it together and look better?"

Our mirrors is where we realize the truth about ourselves. We can either embrace who we are and rejoice in it or reject our beauty and let it affect how we feel. Don't get me wrong—I do use all the anti-aging products, and, yes, I work hard at keeping a positive image of myself and feeling what we all need...loved. Nurturing and caring for ourselves is a necessity in life if we want to feel gratitude when helping others.

You know those horrible sticker name tags that never stick to your clothing and have pre-printed on them, "Hello...My Name is...?" Well, truthfully, some days I look down and make sure my "name tag" in life still says LORI.

Each day you are a new "I AM." The "I AM" you were yesterday doesn't always fit you the same today. You learned, you laughed, you cried, you planned, you interacted with others. You failed, you succeeded, and you brought your heart and story into today. Life is about living in the moments. Some people ask me, "How can you do that?" They mean, how can I embrace today and not be continuously living in the past or planning and anticipating the future? As the stories unfold within the pages of this book, you will understand and see how you can live differently today.

As I breathe in the newness of a bright spring morning, I look back and realize each step has led me to where I am today, not a "life" coach, but a spiritual "visionary" coach. Each morning my "I AM" is to wake up with the intention to hold my clients' hands, hearts, laughter, sometimes anger, sometimes brokenness, and even misdirection in life, and help them "envision" the steps to bring healing, glory, joy, and brilliance back in to their journeys.

It wasn't always this way in my life. It took a while to figure things out and learn to walk my own path, rather than that of someone else.

My husband and I love movies. It is a form of relaxation for us, and sometimes messages will come to me through them. One of those movies is *Nanny McPhee*. In the beginning, the children ask Nanny how long she will be staying there with them. Her reply is profound, "When you need me, but don't WANT me, I will be here. When you want me, but don't NEED me, is when I will leave." That is how I have always felt my "walking" with clients has been. I'm with them as long as they need me. They may not always love the work we do together until they begin truly seeing the path that lies before them. We walk together at their speed with encouragement, understanding, and new awareness, always increasing the pace when they are ready to strengthen their new "I AM's." Endurance, excitement, and confidence are our goals! You can obviously tell I am passionate, not only about my work, but about each client I walk with in their first steps, next steps, and beyond.

As you read or hear the chapters ahead in the "stepping" process, I found my personal "I AM's" on the journey and now walk with them each day as they are ever-evolving. I don't mourn what I have left behind, but rather embrace what I am receiving today and envisioning for tomorrow in my own life and for others.

NOW ASK YOURSELF...*Who am I?*

_____

_____

_____

_____

_____

_____

What is my background and how did I end up becoming a visionary coach?

Have you ever asked yourself, "Why me? Why is my life so hard? Why do I have to go through this difficulty in my life? Why do I feel so alone in everything? Why does she always seem to have it all together, and I don't? Why do I have to feel so bad?" I will be sharing my insights, successes, and challenges further in each of the chapters in hopes of you connecting to my story and those of others.

At one time in my life, I thought I knew who I was and what I did each day in work and in life. I was a therapeutic teacher with a passion for implementing and administering healing work with children, youth, and families. I loved speaking, facilitating, and teaching others to implement positive support for themselves. This started very early for me and continued for over thirty years. Even though the position or the people I served may have changed through the years, the passion I had was intense. I loved working in education and medicine, focusing on learning and behavior with a therapeutic and neuroscience bridge to health care. My work began with children from birth to eight years and continued on to the college aged students, working consistently with families, as well as the medical community, therapists, and educational personnel.

I still love finding new ways to connect with my clients and children. I was an artist and a musician for many years. Music and art are still deeply embedded in my work. My first book was written in my fourth year of teaching, as I taught and facilitated creative lessons and experiences for children. My school district wanted me to teach this to others and urged me to write my book; so, I did. I was honored to speak, facilitate, and shift mind-sets of many individuals working with our youngest of children in many diverse environments. I was known across the state and region as "The Art Lady." So those who know me can now better understand my love for color and all things bright.

As I expanded my work in creativity and positive expression experiences, I would worked collaboratively with therapists, teachers, administrators, organization leaders, hospital personnel, and other support service providers.

Eventually, my platform changed and my work in "sensory connections and brain-based strategies evolved. I would be called into hospitals, schools, universities, or organizations to evoke new ideas and instill motivation, as well as bring solutions to challenges. Through my work as a principal and professor, I strengthened my connections to develop others and highly valued my mission as we witnessed the change in each staff member or student's expanded view of life and of work.

I experienced the "dance" of life, too. Two steps forward… three steps back…one to the side…and KICK. Knowledge and experiences have always been a constant in my life. I found myself always wanting to know more, learn more, practice more, and then share.

In 1999, I received my letter of acceptance for my final degree, PhD, and the journey began. I left my therapeutic classroom job after nineteen years. I couldn't believe I was leaving what I loved to do to pursue this new adventure. My principal gave me my final push with these words when I asked her if I was doing the right thing. She said, "Go where you are needed and where your outreach is the greatest." I have followed those words ever since.

I left the job to add on three more years of school, becoming an administrator and original team member of a new school to be opened on the University of South Florida campus. It was a challenging job while going to school those last couple of years, but so rewarding.

I encountered a significant hurdle when I was completing my PhD. Choosing to move to Texas for an amazing job opportunity was a leap of faith, which I will expand on later. During the last couple of years of data collection, writing, researching, and teaching at the Texas university, I completed everything except the final two chapters when my program was unexpectedly closed due to university changes. It was a very difficult time, and the "two steps backwards" felt much more like "hit the floor." My dream of becoming a doctor of learning and behavior, with a neuroscience focus, was suddenly halted. After much reflection and deep work inside my own heart, I came to realize I was there to expand my work, my knowledge, and my relationships and grow my ability to research and write with purpose. The three letters at the end of my name, and the "Dr." in front of my name weren't important. The experience I gained, however, was priceless.

What do you do? You keep moving forward. I continued my work as a national speaker, not for my own company but an international one. I expanded my methods and strategies by authoring numerous programs, books, and curriculums in my field for the new company. I carried my passion for children, students, and their caregivers, as well as leaders, so each felt positively validated for their strengths and talents. At one point, I supported and coached twenty trainers to facilitate programs in three states. I loved my job! Coaching was key and building relationships was a daily focus. Certified in coaching through one of our very own programs, I was granted the honor to work with such a powerful organization. When passion is present, we soar, even with drastic setbacks.

After becoming a master coach in cognitive, instructional, and emotional coaching, I continued my passion for being an active problem-solver for my clients, employees, and colleagues. Little did I know that later I would be using this for my own company. I would be coaching and expanding this work with a new focus, with even more of myself included. Being armed with knowledge and experience, while pairing these and other certifications in therapy and behavioral supports, proved crucial to the furthering of my journey. My need for being an innovator with a creative flair was only satiated by leading others in new and "out of the box" ways.

While running and traveling with my own company in 2013, life as I knew it came to a massive halt. This was the moment when life changed in a monumental way for me. It was then my responsibilities shifted with the acceptance of my greatest role at that time: to be a full-time caregiver to my elderly mother. Little did I know a new path was being designed for me. After three years of around-the-clock care, my mom gently passed away. This was a devastatingly influential shift in my life.

After the long-term caregiving support of my mother and the onset and development of my own severe chronic illness, I woke up one morning and asked myself, "Why is all of this happening to *me*?" Both experiences had resulted in various forms of grief, and I plunged into that abyss head first. Shortly after, I came to the realization that I needed to make a change.

In the summer of 2015, I prayed for guidance, read, and reflected in order to gain hope and vision for a new beginning. How could I help others using my strengths, knowledge, and abilities, while integrating my newfound insights? Another awakening happened, a new "call to action" occurred in my life and led me to decide to bring forth my spiritual gifts and intuitive abilities to have a deeper impact on others' lives.

Others call my gifts: intuition, prophecy, empathy, medical intuition, and vision. This is probably why I am named the spiritual visionary coach. In some form or another, I have always shared my gifts with others. Yet, this was very new for me, to share my gifts by name. In the past, I used the gifts and abilities I had been given, while spending time gathering experiences and knowledge by acquiring multiple degrees and certifications. I did this to better understand the things I did in my life and work. It was time, however, for me to fully step into my own uniqueness.

Have you ever asked yourself what your gifts are? Most of us do at one time or another in our lives. However, if you would like a little help defining those or support in guiding someone you know in their own pursuit, I can help. Go to our website at walkwithlori.com and download our complimentary "I AM" Personal Profile. Follow the directions and start your journey.

I also suggest using other wonderful resources, such as Marcus Buckingham's StrengthsFinder, our work with Asset-Based Thinking (ABT), and the books by Dr. Kathryn Cramer and Hank Wasiak, entitled *Change the Way You See Everything* and *Change the Way You See Yourself*. There are also wonderful books by Dr. Caroline Leaf, whom I have aligned with over the years, including on her book, *The Gift in You*. These will all assist you with further insights on your own strengths and internal assets.

After the passing of my mother, I took time to process the grief of losing her and of accepting my own recent diagnosis. My way of life would be altered, but I knew it was my time. And I chose to step into my own uniqueness, with confidence and grace, just as I assist others in doing now. That choice led me to the moment where my new path as a visionary and intuitive coaching was revealed to me. I would bring forth new thoughts and ideas in a fresh and impactful way. It was also in that moment that Walk with Lori was created for women to truly re-envision their lives one step at a time, just as I had done in mine. Time to walk out of grief and into hope.

NOW ASK YOURSELF...*What is my background? How do I bring it into my work and everyday life? What gifts do I possess?*

_____
_____
_____
_____

_____
_____
_____
_____

What is my mission and vision now?

I am utterly and completely passionate about helping women to re-envision their lives, one step at a time. It is important for me to see a woman dream big enough for miracles to be manifested. When each of us to take a different look at what we have, what we want, and what we are doing to make it happen, change and transformation takes place. I have been there myself, and continue to reexamine my life and purpose around every turn and twist.

How can I give you hope in your walk? I have walked many of these same roads and continue to do so, only now from a stronger, wiser, and more understanding perspective. Walking a similar path, however, is not enough sometimes. We must bring our experience and knowledge with us.

After much reflection and actually walking, living, and stumbling in this process, I can now answer the ultimate question of…Who am I? In the book *Behind Her Brand*, I share how embracing the I AM of your life is the most powerful knowledge and belief you can put into practice to be successful and influence others.

I believe our I AM changes our path, our perceptions. Here are my I AM statements and their alignment to my current blessings of abundance and success.

- ♥ I AM a visionary risk-taker. As a visionary, I believe there are unique opportunities for us to grasp to change our world. I believe in changing the world one view and one action at a time. This belief allows me the freedom to assist others in their new glimpse of life with no fear or lack, only challenges and solutions.

- ♥ I AM a heart and soul-led, relationship-driven connector. I believe in each person's unique work and their uninterrupted pursuit of happiness in life and work. Whether I am on a team, working with an individual, or connecting with a group, all strengths and talents are to be celebrated and embraced. Synergy occurs when two or more forces work together to produce an effect greater than the total of their own separate results.

  Sometimes it is a difficult situation when I find myself in a team or collaborative partnership that isn't following a mission aligned with these concepts. It is my believe I have to honor them and myself by sometimes walking away or connecting them with someone else to complete their own "path" of purpose. It is about staying true to God, self, and others.

- ♥ I AM passionately motivated and lovingly intentional. This is where my drive to pursue my goals and actions each day lies. As an entrepreneur and leader, I work diligently to instill the desire to have an intention or purpose for the day, a way to measure it, an action to celebrate it, and a breath to be grateful for it.

- ♥ I AM purposefully knowledgeable. Learning has always been at the heart of my career, whether it was earning a degree, participating in professional learning, attending conferences, writing books, or networking with groups of colleagues to discover new ways of thinking. It is what keeps us fresh in our fields and allows us to have the ability to share with others our own achievements, experiences, and predictions.

You are outrageously unique and the next step of your path is waiting for you. I know I can't wait!

NOW ASK YOURSELF...*What is my mission in life or a vision of what I desire? What are my I AM's?*

_____
_____
_____
_____
_____
_____
_____

How did I end up on reality TV? How did it all begin?

You may even already know me as a visionary coach and therapist on *The Real Housewives of Dallas*. How did it all happen? Did I interview for the position? Did I know someone? Why was I chosen?

Do you believe in synchronicity? Synchronicity is a concept explaining how events are meaningful coincidences. Do you ever feel like things just happen for a reason or due to some miracle? If you said "yes," you will believe me when I tell you I never thought I would follow a path that would lead to me working and appearing on *The Real Housewives of Dallas*. Do you want to know what really happened?

In April 2016, I took a call from a colleague who knew I was a national speaker sharing a positive and motivational message. They needed a speaker for an upcoming event supporting women in transition through a local nonprofit charity. After taking a break from traveling due to my health and family responsibilities, I had started speaking again on my journey of overcoming chronic illness. The audience was comprised of women and my personal focus of transformation and triumph was welcomed.

What a fabulous way to come back into my passion! I felt "called" into action again.

It was a day of glamour and beauty for the women, paired with my interactive message of "steps." Among many welcoming women asking for insight and motivation into their situations of starting over and job loss, was the celebrity who was the epitome of beauty, a "housewife" of Dallas. While sharing ideas and interactions with the participants, I got vulnerable and exposed my own walk. Somehow my message caught the interest of our celebrity that day. It was at that moment I started my path to becoming "housewife" Stephanie Hollman's visionary coach. Stephanie was experiencing what we do when life and relationships are involved. She had a friendship crisis on her heart that involved a very dear friend and fellow "housewife," Brandi Redmond.

She was mourning the loss of a "sister" in her life. Our work together focused on empowering her to be the best version of herself.

Things happen when we show up. Opportunities present themselves when we step out. In July 2016, I was attending an entrepreneurial retreat for growing a business exponentially with my national business coach, Bill Walsh. We were asked to write down a vision statement so large we either scared ourselves or laughed at the possibility, maybe even both. John Maxwell calls it "dreaming so big that only God can rush to make it happen."

I took a big breath and wrote, "to breathe life into the vision of delivering a call for a million women to re-envision their lives while leaving their own legacy of love and hope for others." Wow, a million women! What was I thinking? What could possibly compel me to draft a vision that left me giddy with excitement, yet breathless with fear. Was it a belief in something greater at work? I choose to call them miracles of God. In late August 2016, thirty days after writing my vision statement, I was asked to be on the Real Housewives of Dallas. This was one of those moments that created a seismic shift in my outreach and ability to support more women nationally in their search for purpose. Who knows? Maybe even a million! What did I do next? I wrote a NEW and even bigger vision statement, of course!

NOW ASK YOURSELF...What moments have I had in synchronicity or coincidence that shifted my life? What dreams are so BIG they scare me?

_____
_____
_____
_____
_____
_____
_____

Why have I chosen to write this book?

My heart's desire is to see women empowered, equipped, and walking out their destinies as they impact and influence our world. Are you ready and open to learn and experience more from your life? Would you enjoy having more "get-to" experiences than "have to's?" Or are you stuck in your current "steps" due to health, job, family responsibilities, financial constraints, or even emotional wounds? I truly understand. I was once there too. Do you want something else in life and you just keep experiencing the same old thing? How do you shift to new outcomes and possibilities? I will supply answers to those questions for you as we explore deeper in later chapters.

Writing this book has been very important to me. For three years I walked the practical steps of stepping out, stepping up, and stepping forward in my personal journey. It is my belief that I was meant to step ahead, gain insights, and share them with YOU.

One of those insights is that life must be about balance and bliss. For me, moments spent in balance and feeling blissful would include retail therapy, especially when it involves shoes. It could include a night out with friends, a hot bubble bath, and a favorite treat or beverage or laughing until you cry. It is important to find a healthy balance between responsibilities, taking care of our own health, and sometimes the health and wellness of those in our care. It is a moment in which we are allowing the opportunities to be let go and enjoy life.

There are times when we have to reestablish what fun looks like in our life. We may have spent time and energy taking care of others or managing all the "have to's" on our plates, we have lost our true sense of self. How about you? What types of things do you consider to be fun? What would put a smile on your face?

NOW ASK YOURSELF...Have you ever thought your life would become a fabulous story? Have you ever journaled or written about your life? What aspects of your story would you want to share?

_____
_____
_____
_____
_____
_____
_____

chapter two
The Importance in Our Steps

*"Faith is taking the first step
even when you don't see the staircase."*
—Martin Luther King, Jr.

The steps we take are a reflection of the life we have lived and how we desire to live in the future. Steps have always been an important aspect of our lives, from baby steps to steps down an aisle on your wedding day. Our steps are meant to help us grow and develop as we continue along our paths in life.

My husband and I have four grandchildren. We are incredibly blessed with three girls and one boy who are deeply rooted in our hearts. We also believe at any time this could change with more additions. Our love will only continue to expand accordingly. Little did I know how precious steps were until I truly stood back and watched. As a nana, carrying those sweet little babies required the gentlest of steps. I walked the floor to lull them to sleep. I paced the floor while they were crying or not feeling well. I tiptoed past their bedrooms to ensure a restful sleep. I carried them upstairs for nap time or playtime, with steps of sure-footing. As I saw them take their own first steps, paired with falling I felt each step. They learned to pick themselves back up again. This is reminiscent of the process we all must face: the first steps, then walking, running, climbing, and thriving. These movements were all with a helpful hand of reassurance.

My husband and I recognize the importance of our steps. Watching our granddaughters walking with their friends and our youngest grandchildren walking, giggling and jumping too. Stepping ahead of us in their exuberance for life. We see it with our own children. Walking with their spouses in the cadence of unison steps. Moving into the rhythm of walking as family. Mostly, we feel it in our slowing of steps as we are getting older, and the conversations around our growing sense of how each step affects the steps of our expanding family.

Each of these steps is filled with unique challenges and "cheers." Yet, we can learn so much from observing and appreciating how we get there.

In life, our steps are powerful. One of my friends is a mom to four beautiful children. When her fourth child began to take her first steps, she noticed something peculiar. Her baby girl was walking on her tiptoes. This continued throughout her toddler years. In fact, she never did learn to walk flat-footed, feet securely on the ground, until she was about three and a half. Even then, she would occasionally revert back to her comfortable, tiptoed gait, because this was what felt natural to this sweet little girl.

Today, at thirteen, she moves her mother to tears with her beautiful choreography. It's as if the world stands still for those few minutes and all of heaven awaits to see what beauty will pour out from her heart. There is no doubt that from the beginning, this gift had been woven into the fabric of her DNA. While some would have viewed her tiptoed walking as an abnormality, she felt secure, free, and accomplished learning to walk and balance her own tiptoed steps. Today those steps are leading her toward her destiny.

Look within yourself and see the steps you might choose to take. We have steps of creativity, opportunity, faith, hope, and love. There are steps of walking away and walking toward and pausing without walking at all. As we continue the journey, emotions and experiences should be valued. The steps we take strengthen our faith and resolve to continue the journey, no matter where it is going.

For a moment, I would like to bring you on one of my walks with family.

One day, our son came home with a sweet young girl whom he had worked with while going to college. That sounds like a normal occasion, yet for him it wasn't. He had wonderful girls that were friends, and we had met many of those during the typical parties and special events. She, however, was unique. They were heading out to the lake for some fun on the jet skis and had dropped in to grab a few things. His steps were different with her. He walked gently, held the door for her, and protected her as he escorted her into the vehicle to drive away. We saw it! The steps of love were in motion. Those were the first steps that would lead to many other "firsts" in their lives.

Within a couple of years, their steps changed again. We watched them walk down a grassy path surrounded by rows of beautifully decorated white chairs. His steps were with purpose and conviction, dedication, and a little excitement. His heart prepared to accept the greatest mission—that of a husband. Her steps were taken with joy and in fervent belief that they were each other's love mates for life. We all knew it as we watched them take those steps toward each other. It was as if they were the only two people standing on the stairs of the white gazebo at sunset.

The next steps were in joy, as they moved into their first home and then found themselves dancing with excitement over the news that they were going to have a baby. We couldn't believe it! My husband and I were going to be grandparents again, and we were ready!

Now walk with me for just a minute, as I bring you into a

frozen moment in time. That place where your mind takes a snapshot, or creates a video clip. That place in your mind that is replaying a moment over and over. When the rest of the world gets quiet, it is that moment when you've realized that a true transition has taken place, right before your eyes. The crossover that happens when we move from being a couple to being parents, being parents to becoming grandparents. If you blink, you might miss the subtle breath between these transitions. It is in those special moments when you've recognized they have taken yet another step.

With each passing day, our son had been there for our daughter-in-love's pregnancy, from cravings to vomiting to tears and fears to laughter and preparations. He was walking step by step in unison with her.

One particular evening she was experiencing contractions. They called the OB doctor and were told to drive to the hospital to get checked. Based on past "false alarms," neither of our kids thought she was going to stay, but it was better to be safe than being sorry.

When they checked in, the doctor on duty let them know that it was real this time. Our little mommy to-be, was progressing very slowly. At three a.m. they called to let us know we probably should come on up to the hospital. We packed and brought what we needed to stay. After what seemed like many hours, her labor stalled in progression. This caused the pain to present an even more exhausting challenge on their already depleted energy supply. To restart the labor process, the doctor and floor nurses suggested our kids walk around the circular configuration of the floor.

As they started their walk around, our son cradled our daughter-in-love into his protective arms. He supported her uncomfortable body and painful back and shoulders as she waddled around on swollen, exhausted feet, taking small steps forward. They would both smile slightly, overwhelmed with joy, yet focused on what was happening to them very soon. The steps to parenthood flooded their minds, anticipating the birth of a small little angel who would soon call them "mommy" and "daddy." With each lap they made, we were blessed to witness the loving exchanges they shared.

He took intentional steps around the floor and we watched our son become a dad. His ability to nurture, protect, and strengthen our daughter-in-love created a comfort and confidence that no matter how long this labor was going to be, he was fully invested, now and forever going forward. He was already committed to their marriage and was a terrific husband and a fabulous stepdad. This was different. We all saw it. He was realizing the next chapter in their lives. He faced it with intention and purpose, wanting to be completely ready.

> Steps of intention and transition are necessary to walk into new life.

He claimed his new role as he upheld his wife in her steps of pregnancy and now in her labor. They were becoming stronger together and we knew it! Most importantly, so did they. Their smiles became bigger, and eventually the walking ended. The next chapter began. Our grandson, the first boy, was born! Steps made with intention and transition are necessary to walk into new life.

Early in my career, one of my students took steps that changed me forever. Some of the best years in my career were spent working with young children, ages three to five, with unique and varying exceptionalities. My students presented these challenges in learning, behavioral, and physical abilities, and sometimes a combination of all of these. I loved learning and finding ways to connect to where they were at and anticipate what their needs were by using numerous therapeutic deliveries, which included music, art, movement, physical, occupational, and speech/language, all through the common learning modality of PLAY.

Much of the time, I think I learned more from my students than they did from me, and this little girl was one of my greatest teachers. She came into my classroom when she had just turned three years old. Her radiant smile gave us our first introduction. Then, I met her mom and could quickly discern why.

They were just alike! Motivated, inspired, and vivacious. She had a rare disorder that also presented itself as spina bifida, as well as other cognitive and language difficulties. The doctors had shared with her mom and dad heartbreaking news that she would probably never walk, stand, or be able to take care of herself as she got older. They chose, however, not to let anyone put limits on their daughter's capabilities. They learned to live in each day and celebrate it to the fullest. For them, every small success was a significant one. I ran my classroom and all its experiences the same way. We were destined to be working together on this very belief. Little did we know, she, in her own way, would teach us the greatest lesson.

Our therapy team worked in the classroom every day. They each collaborated with me assessing the medical and physical challenges of our precious students. We would then create positive interactions and connections to life and learning every day. As we all delved into assessment of this little girl, the news regarding her prognosis was difficult to hear. We would only take the information of her case into consideration. Surprisingly, she had her own thoughts and feelings about herself.

One morning, her mom brought her in and we chatted for a while about the upcoming holiday parties. She volunteered a lot and we were planning something special for the children. Chelsea may have been playing nearby, but she was listening the whole time. After her mom left, she scooted herself over on the floor using her little combat crawl, which was a new achievement for her. She looked up at me and said, "Ms. Lori, I want to do something for Mommy and Daddy for Christmas." I, of course, was thinking she meant creating something special for them because she thoroughly enjoyed creative expression. She then proceeded to tell me, "I want to walk out to breakfast on Christmas morning." You could have heard a pin drop, or maybe that was my jaw hitting the floor. How could I possibly say to this little three-year-old that walking out, on her own, or even standing up, was an unrealistic goal, especially since it was already November 1st? It had taken us since August to even work with her on combat crawling and that in itself was very new.

What would I do? I told her we would focus all our energy on strengthening, stabilizing, and giving her the ability to take steps for her to present her "gift" to her parents. Then, she added, "Oh…I don't want Mommy to know we are working on this, either." Mic drop! I agreed to her plan, and later, while my little ones were taking their afternoon rest time, I gathered the therapists together and shared my dilemma with them. They all thought I had gone completely crazy and even said I was delusional to give her my promise to participate in her plan.

Was she delusional? Was I? What would you have told her? Would you have said, "No, you will never walk. Should I only set a goal or intention that isn't too far out of reach to ensure that she could achieve it?" Well, I couldn't and wouldn't do that. Instead, we created a plan toward her special gift for her family and we worked every day until she was so tired she couldn't even combat crawl. She pushed and pushed, never giving up on the goal of the gift she longed to share with her parents. We designed all her other therapies and learning to contain a physical component to them. We were always working toward the goal. I was exhausted and so was she! There were times I couldn't believe I agreed to this desire. Did I set her up for failure or did I give her unrealistic hope? I didn't think so. There was so much learning and growth taking place, and as a result, extensive strength and character was being built!

Before we knew it, December was here. It was time for the holiday party. Her mom was an integral part of the celebration for everyone. We decorated, baked, and planned it to be an amazing day. All of the kids and families had a wonderful time. Chelsea moved around the room combat crawling and letting us carry her a little in between, just as we usually would do. I had still not seen her walk or even stand on her own yet and neither had any of the therapists. We were concerned about what was going to happen. Before she left for the holiday, I managed to have her help me deliver treats to the school staff, while she sat in a wagon and handed them all out. As we finished the last one, I sat down with her and asked if she was ready for whatever was going to happen over the holiday with her gift for mommy and daddy.

She smiled and said, "Ms. Lori, please don't worry. Even if I can't walk, I am so much stronger and doing a lot now. Mommy and Daddy will be happy." She was absolutely right! Why did I doubt her?

On Christmas morning, I could feel that Chelsea was planning something. That morning, my husband and I were having breakfast before preparing for family dinner. It was still pretty early. Our phone rang, and I knew it was Penny, Chelsea's mom. I took a deep breath and thought of all the time, energy, and effort we all put behind one young child's dream. God...wouldn't it be wonderful if...Could I let myself even pray that prayer? Did I believe it could actually be true? Just for a brief moment, I could. I picked up the phone, and it wasn't Penny, but her husband. I could hear Chelsea laughing and talking in the background in her sweet way. "Lori, this is Don, could you come over for just a little bit? We have a Christmas gift for you and Chelsea wanted to give it to you herself." I was perplexed. This was strange. I agreed to come over for coffee and my husband was supportive of a break in the morning before we were to have holiday meals and family events to attend to later. I quickly got dressed, wondering the whole time if anything had happened. Did she even try to show something to them after all of her hard work?

As I drove over to the house, I will admit my heart was a little heavy. Sometimes it is difficult when you want something to happen so badly and it isn't a possibility. I loved my job! It was my calling. Yet, my heart was always involved and deeply invested in each step taken and not taken. I parked the car and walked slowly up the stairs to the front door. Penny and Don greeted me with a Merry Christmas hug and an overwhelming welcome, as usual. I walked into the kitchen, where they had already poured me a cup of coffee and we sat down to chat. They said I had a gift to open and then called Chelsea to come out from her room, so we could open it. I will never forget the image I witnessed that day!

"I'm coming, Ms. Lori," but I turned around to watch her standing up, holding the wall, and taking her first of many steps toward me. I couldn't believe the miracle of those steps...the beauty in the balance, strength, and placement of each foot...one at a time being laid down on the floor. The most radiant smile of pure joy adorned her sweet face. I didn't know whether I was going to cry or jump up and dance, so I did both. As a matter of fact, we all did! Penny and Don then shared with me what happened. Early that morning their door opened, and a little girl, still in her pajamas, was standing there with the hall light illuminating her gift, as if it were on display for all to see. With only a silhouette standing in the doorway, taking a few steps toward their bed, they both thought they were dreaming. They said out loud, "Chelsea?" She then started giggling so hard and excitedly that she fell over on the floor laughing hysterically. They jumped up, and she said, "No, I'm not done showing you my present." She pulled herself up and teetered over to them sitting on the bed. It was the best day ever! I was so honored they shared it with me. So blessed to be a part of watching a child's dream reach something bigger than any of us could have imagined. We witnessed the tremendous gift of first steps, the power of persistence in steps, of steps toward a new reality in life, and the determination of achieving those steps for those we love most dearly.

What steps matter to you in your life? What steps do you honor? Which ones erupt a feeling of reservation or even fear? Do your steps have hope and healing in them or hurt and harm? Steps have the ability to strengthen and enhance our lives, as well as steal our breath, along with the ability to step forward, with faith, with love.

What is your favorite memory of important steps taken?

By now you know, I adore watching children in their moments of curiosity, connection, and wonder about the world around them. Another treasured experience I had was with a friend's very young child who was, could we say, obsessed with shoes. At two years old, where most children would have a drawer or a cabinet filled with toys, she had one filled with shoes. For each social event, outing, or holiday, when asked what to buy her, it was always shoes. One afternoon, I happened to be babysitting for my friend. When Jazz awoke from her nap, I picked her up out of her crib, and she motioned for me to sit down on the floor with her. I looked down at her with a smile as I waited to see what we were going to play. Little did I know we were opening this large drawer of shoes of all colors, textures, and for many different occasions. She had ruby slippers with sequins, beach thongs with shells, ballet shoes with ribbons, and black patent leather party shoes with a big silver buckle. She began pulling one shoe out at a time and handing them to me. As she shared her prized possessions, we searched for their mates, and lined them up carefully on the soft rug. I could tell there was a story about each pair, and imagined it to be where she wore them, what outfit they accompanied, and where she may be going. We completed all the mates and as we finished, she uttered a sigh of joy and satisfaction. We carefully placed them back into her drawer and closed it up for another day. This was a special moment because she shared what was important to her with me. To this day, she dresses in a unique way, and with a pair of carefully chosen shoes. Her shoes show everyone, "I am me."

I would like to think that the steps she took in each of those shoes were so honored and filled with self-confidence. Each step taken would have its own meaning. I knew she was a child after my own heart. Ah, the love of shoes!

What is it about shoes and steps? First, I LOVE SHOES, always have and always will. We will take steps in our lives that carry so much meaning in our hearts. We will take positive steps in creativity, opportunity, faith, hope, and love. We will take challenging steps in loss, lack, and lessons. Each step will have its own set of emotions and transformations.

Do you embrace your steps of transformation? Whose steps do you see when you close your eyes? Are they walking with you, away from you, toward you? Each of those images will happen to us, and understanding them, appreciating them, blessing them, and feeling excitement and acceptance about them changes our journey.

We can close our eyes and see how we all have a unique cadence, rhythm, and walk. When I pick up my husband from the airport, no matter how far away he is from me, I can recognize his methodical steps as he comes closer and closer into view. After twelve years together, he still makes my heart jump and I'm happy he is home. Our son, Luke, walks more and more like his dad and it is such a special sight.

I was blessed to learn so much in my early life from my parents and extended family. My dad was my hero and guardian in life. He retired as a general in the Army National Guard and was chief of staff for the State of Illinois for a very long time. Dad was a passionate leader of his men and a role model to many with an unwavering commitment to those who knew him. He was a lay leader in our church and his deep faith came early on in his life. As a chaplain in the Coast Guard and a Sunday school teacher became pivotal mentors in his life and grounded his steps to become the man he would become. He didn't have a strong family support system. Dad always had a dream in life of creating a family with enough love and support that we could do anything. Growing up, Dad was always involved in our lives even with traveling and working as much as he did. As a child I remember picking him up from the airport (as I do now with my own husband) and running up to every man in uniform because all I saw were legs. Yet, as I grew, I knew his steps! I couldn't wait to have him home and share my most recent escapades with him.

When I was only twenty-four, I lost my dad. It was one of the most difficult events in my life. To this day, his intelligence and inner wisdom remain in my heart and mind. I am now the age my father was when he passed away, and I realize how precious life is every day.

Dad was known for participating in maneuvers with his battalions long after he was required to participate. He knew walking alongside his men gave them motivation and a feeling of intense support. His steps were very important to him and the impact each made was part of Dad's focus and mission, especially with me.

His steps would change forever, and I do believe this became one of the reasons he retired early and decided to spend his life with my mom and me walking on the beach in Florida.

During my freshman year of high school, I was working my very first job as a waitress. It was a Friday night and my parents always golfed with friends. One of my parents' dear friends came into the restaurant and we were very busy. I came over to greet them. Their faces said everything. They were bringing me a difficult message, so I wouldn't have to hear it over a phone.

My dad had been in a severe golf cart accident and was taken to the hospital. While Dad was trying to chip his ball on the green, the cart had stalled on a steep incline. The brake didn't hold and the cart began careening down the hill towards him. He did not have time to move away. My dad rolled with the golf cart down the hill into a deep ravine and was pinned by the heavy engine part on his chest, just below his heart. Everyone in their golf party, including my mom, watched in fear and disbelief of what was happening. Dad's leg was shattered in four places and they were concerned that there was internal damage of his organs. As I heard the news, I was in shock and the most difficult part was my parents wanted me to finish out my shift and go home at the end of the evening. What? Not go to the hospital? My dad was in critical condition!

Thank goodness the worst injuries were to his leg, not internally. After a long surgery, Dad's leg was pinned and grafted together, forever altering his steps in life. The pain which followed during therapy and forward, made him realize the preciousness of making each moment count. My own life was changed. Alongside my mom, I would be his supportive caregiver and help with his recuperation process. As he healed, I learned, firsthand, how each step in our lives can be either endured or embraced. Dad chose to embrace and little by little he was able to walk again. We were blessed with him in our lives for a little while longer.

Each step matters. Many of my clients reflect and share about the steps they've made in life—the ones they celebrate and the ones they would like to sometimes forget. I will continue to share insights, stories, and reflections from my own life and my work, including the "housewives."

At the end of each chapter, you will be given questions for you to interact with and that encourage you to take your steps and transform.

You may choose to use the companion journal to deepen your own "walk."

Trust the process and hear how your brilliance comes from seeing who you really ARE and bringing HER with you. We want you to truly see your own "I AM" and realize SHE is AMAZING! She is a woman who is "stepping OUT, stepping UP, stepping FORWARD, and envisioning leaping." You are that woman! Are you ready to take your next steps? Let's get started!

> *Walk with Lori: Your Steps of Importance*
>
> What are your favorite shoes? Why? Is it for comfort, style, support, or for another reason?
>
> Whose steps do you see in your journey? How are they a part of your walk?
>
> How would you define your steps in life: labored, joyful, appreciative, heavy, or methodical? Why?
>
> What steps would you like to be experiencing? In what areas of your life?
>
> What steps are your greatest challenge?

To increase your "walk" with Lori even further, you will want to purchase the companion workbook and journal at WalkWithLori.com.

chapter three
Step OUT: The Comfort Zone

*"Courageously surrender to your passion...
magnificence will be born."*
—Ellie Drake, BraveHeart Women

*"When you want something, all the powers and things in the
universe, come together to help you achieve it!"*
—Paulo Coelho, The Alchemist

It's Saturday, and the house is quiet. I lie in bed with the alarm turned off, cuddling with my two sweet kittens. I hear the stillness of our home, no sounds except the inhale and exhale rhythm of my own breathing. Nothing on my calendar today restricts me from the freedom to stay in my pajamas and just rest. Reading, writing, watching movies, and cooking will be my pursuits today.

Is this the comfort zone? For me, sometimes it is. How would most of the population define *comfort zone*? Everyone talks about it; we have all been in it. Yet what is it? Is it really a negative thing in our lives that we should avoid? I want to explore the concept that it can be both positive AND negative.

Comfort Zone: A Positive or Negative Space

A comfort zone is defined as "a place or situation where one feels safe or at ease and without stress." Looking at this definition, it would seem we embrace all the benefits by staying *within* our comfort zones as a time to "press pause," heal, and readjust. In doing so, we gain the tools necessary to move forward in a successful and purposeful way.

Why do we all love the comfort zone? In this space, we are not experiencing stress or pushing ourselves to do more. We are just *being*...not too hot, not too cold, but just right. We struggle to step out of the comfort zone because we are wired to seek out comfort, just as a young child looks for a hug when they fall. It is a natural and neutral state for us to live in, where stress and anxiety are at their lowest points. It allows us to regroup and plan our next steps.

How would *you* define *your* comfort zone? Is it short term, maybe a few hours or even a day, just to allow you to regroup? Or is it a month of feeling immobilized, stuck in an abyss of utter lack, with no joy or passion to be found? Do you judge yourself in the comfort zone? What may your mind, body, and spirit be craving? Could it just be a moment of self-care spent on a soft couch, curled up with a good book or watching a great movie? I personally love the spa-infused bath time I create it with candles, music, and an all-natural bath bomb. It is one hour of pure bliss! It nurtures my mind, body, and spirit through sensory channels and allows my brain and body to reconnect in a healing manner. Yoga and meditation are other self-care daily practices of mine. What are yours?

Being in a place of comfort has somehow become the center of negative conversations with others when, truthfully, it serves as a place of safety for us when needed. Some of my clients have shared their comfort zone experiences as:

- ♥ Hibernation
- ♥ Pizza and ice cream moments
- ♥ Time in "the cave"
- ♥ Perpetual spa days
- ♥ Depression in bed

Below are the heartfelt responses from numerous women I queried on their own feelings of the comfort zone. Look at how diverse their comments appear. See if you find your own feelings or experiences somewhere within their words. Then, take a moment at the end of the chapter or in the companion journal to reflect and write your own illustration and narrative.

- ♥ *I live outside of my comfort zone almost daily. My comfort zone is anywhere I am with my husband. He's my source of strength, and this is where I go to recharge.*
- ♥ *My comfort zone is usually being with people I'm close to and who I know care about me—people who allow me the freedom to say what's on my mind—good or bad. It can also be a book or something I'm watching, where I can remove myself from inner or outer turmoil and "turn things off" for a while.*
- ♥ *The comfort zone is where we can just "slide" through life, content and knowing we will be okay. But, I know to be great, I HAVE to step out of that comfort zone.*
- ♥ *At least for me, my comfort zone is when I am in a routine. Circles, however, only cause us to end up where we started. So, I must shift my routine to achieve growth.*
- ♥ *My comfort zone has become that place where I am feeling stretched and somewhat **un**comfortable. Ha! So much growth has made "uncomfortable" a more*

comfortable place for me.

- ♥ My comfort zone is where I am most familiar. It's literally where I can go and not have to think. This is a very robotic place. The older I get, the more I want to live in and walk in my purpose. I have become increasingly uncomfortable in my comfort zone. It is simply no longer enough.
- ♥ My comfort zone is when I am "moving." Providing I am solving something or making progress, I feel good. Indecision and stagnation are things that make my anxiety levels climb!! I am trying to learn to relax, to find comfort and peace in the "not knowing." (Dang it's hard!)
- ♥ My comfort zone is being able to do a task in my sleep. I get bored very easily, because I don't grow when I'm in my comfort zone. So, it's necessary for me to seek to do the impossible so that I can participate in the transformation of God in my life.
- ♥ My comfort zone is when I am at ease with myself, when I remain believing that all is well and I'm right where I am supposed to be. Here, nothing outside of me can define or disrupt my existence.
- ♥ The comfort zone is that place where I'm not self-critical, comparing myself to others and seeing myself as "less than." It's the place where I am flying high, yet grounded; solid like a rock. It's the place where I accept myself for the timeline I'm on, and I work to be aligned with the one true source. It's being in nature, drumming, and singing to the heavens. It's providing myself the space to be me! No negotiations.
- ♥ I don't really like being in my comfort zone for too long. Yes, it is a safe place, and I welcome it sometimes. However, it also causes me the most angst. The need for growth is a huge part of my well-being.
- ♥ Comfort zone, for me, is the place where everything is

as it should be. There are no bumps, no lumps and no growth. You ask nothing of yourself beyond what you are absolutely certain you can do well. I have mixed emotions about my comfort zone. Too often, I can see the potential and then chastise myself for not venturing out to grasp a piece of that potential. Other times, however, that leap can be very devastating, and it proves wise not to step out. I sometimes have issues with that balance.

- *A comfort zone??? Well, my comfort zone very rarely happens on its own, but when it does, it is because I feel God's embrace holding me close. It is truly the best! For example, when I get lost in His majestic night sky and think about how He named every star and planet, I am in awe. He touched each one for me. Or it might be in the ripple of creek water cascading over rocks as it flows downstream toward its final kiss to the mouth of a river. The tranquility of both soothes my soul!*
- *I like to start and end my day in my comfort zone, snuggled next to my honey. When he's not around, I start and end my day in silence snuggled in a blanket, bringing a similar effect. Other comfort zones come and go. I like taking calculated risks, learning to build structured plans, while continuing to watch for pitfalls. I've seen through my work that disaster or others can destroy your home, financial security, family, career, etc. So, it's good to roll with what you have now, make room for more to come, and give thanks every night for the good that presented itself that day.*
- *My comfort zone is a safe and warm place. However, when I am stretched, poked, or dance dangerously outside this zone…that's when I get my breakthrough!*

These responses offer you an inside look at how some would describe their comfort zones. Could you relate at all? These participants were questioned even further when asked, "Would you view your comfort zone as a positive or a negative space?" Some individuals describe it as negative. Could this be due to the comments we have heard, such as, "Life begins at the end of your comfort zone?" As you will read in Chapter 4, I believe we must nurture ourselves by a balance of "BEING" and "DOING" to experience the greatest joy and happiness in life. BEING includes time to be still and quiet. It involves healing, learning, meditating, and listening. Isn't that what the comfort zone is doing for us? Any experience can turn negative if we stay too long or participate in things that are harmful to our growth, such as self-medicating. It's how you approach the comfort zone activities and your personal mindset that determine a positive or negative outcome. How we perceive our comfort zones and whether they are healthy places to heal or spaces for self-sabotage is the question. Hurting without resolution and hiding what truly needs to be realized and released will prove counterproductive. This is *not* the treasure that can be found within the comfort zone experience.

Lessons Learned from The Real Housewives of Dallas

If you are a *The Real Housewives of Dallas* (RHOD) fan and watch Season 2 of the show, you witnessed Stephanie walk through disillusionment, being judged unjustly by a friend. Brandi was not just a casual acquaintance either; she was Stephanie's best friend. When we listen too intently to a friend and their needs, it's possible to overwhelm ourselves with their pain and even carry it as our own. Their lessons in life become our lessons. Their struggles and challenges become ours. If we don't unplug periodically and give ourselves the self-care and consistent balance we need, we are not able to fill back up and continue giving to others. This is what Stephanie began experiencing in her life and her close relationship with Brandi. Brandi was going through some toxic challenges, and the only person she could confide in, besides her mom, was her best friend. Women need those safe, intimate friendships, having someone come alongside us as we work through our hurdles to turn them into "highlights." Brandi was balancing a great deal…the new "spotlight," her children, her marriage, volunteering, and her philanthropy work. She and Stephanie had been friends for a very long time and their husbands also remained close friends. Their children had even been purposely born very close to one another, so they would have an additional connection in life.

It's possible, at times, to feel so close to a friend yet not understand them at the same time. How does this occur? Well, it happens to all of us. You might have experienced a genuine desire to be there for a friend, yet felt unable to deliver at the expense of your own responsibilities and life roles. When the argument occurred with Brandi and Stephanie, there was no true discussion or incident that resulted in the lack of connection between them. Stephanie could simply tell Brandi was extremely upset with her. Their daily phone calls and texts had come to a complete halt. You can imagine the feeling of "lack" Stephanie experienced. She even equated it to suffering from the "death" of a friend. The only difference was, in death, the other person isn't on social media making the distance between them obvious to everyone they both knew. Brandi was showing Stephanie that she had moved on and was enjoying it, while posting negative statements about both their former friendship and Stephanie as a person. How painful to watch this all unfold! What could have happened to create such a drastic wedge between them? Often for the other person, the outcome of our pulling away from them as we heal from exhaustion and energy depletion can feel like a disconnect. That is exactly what happened. With Stephanie's absence and change from the way she had always been, Brandi felt offended. She voiced to others, "How could she not be there for me?" She began seeing Stephanie and her actions through the tainted lenses of offense. As a result, the situation remained unresolved for four to five months, even though it seemed like an eternity.

As Stephanie and I began working together, she shared how the needs and responsibilities in the friendship became overwhelming, resulting in emotional and mental exhaustion. She is a true "feeler" and a strong empathetic person, which can result in energy depletion. Those of you who are considered "feelers" may relate to Stephanie's situation. You are compassionate, sometimes to a fault, as you risk losing your own balance to help others through their challenges. You may take on too much, seeing the need *in* and *for* others, and rise to the occasion to be truly present for someone else. You feel much more comfortable as a giver than a receiver. It is challenging for feelers to maintain energy. Therefore, remembering to engage in self-care is essential to your continued balance. Does this sound anything like you?

Challenges have a way of showing us the panoramic view of our lives, and the intersecting relationships and actions along the way. Stephanie realized in their time apart that she needed time for herself to "fill back up" from the overwhelming stress and energy required to support her dear friend. In doing so, however, Brandi felt the lack of positive energy in her life. Brandi then began seeing everything through the lens of perceived rejection by a friend who couldn't be there for her in the way she wanted. When our friends are in a place of "lack" in life, many times we attempt to fill the gap. In other words, instead of empowering them to see the lessons and gather new strengths and tools, we enable them. We give them no need to learn the "bigger" lessons in life, feeling as if we are protecting them instead. Stephanie was accustomed to doing just that. However, in trying to fulfill all her roles and deal with some difficult changes and circumstances in her own life, she crash landed into a feeling of being empty. When we are empty of energy and rely only on our own ability to be filled back up, we end up in the depths of the comfort zone. For Stephanie, this resulted in depression.

At the time, Stephanie was feeling torn by her increased desire to be there for her friend and her personal family struggle with her son's educational progress. As you may know, Stephanie's youngest son wasn't learning and progressing at the same level his classmates were during his first-grade year. His teachers were concerned, frequently alerting Stephanie and her husband, Travis, to the situation. How could she handle the growing needs of her child at the level required, along with all her other existing responsibilities, and still be there for Brandi? Travis, himself, had been challenged by dyslexia and the struggle was just beginning for their young child. They needed to embrace his learning differences and research the best possible place for his positive growth and development, along with the emotional aspects arising with the change in school environments. His older brother was excelling and would be staying at the current school, while he would be moving elsewhere. It was time for the family to go and visit schools and evaluate programs, therapies, and new routines to give him the very best options for his next steps in life. This would all take significant time and effort. Stephanie questioned how Brandi would ever understand how vital it was for her to attend to this family need.

The feelings of guilt and shame were ever present in her mind. The questions rolled in like a flood. Had she neglected her "mom" duties and not been there for her son? Should she have seen his uniqueness and challenges sooner? Did her support of a friend take precedence over her family? How can we, as women, balance our many responsibilities and commitments in life? As Stephanie found out more about her son's needs, the guilt she felt increased. Inadequacy in all aspects of her life crept into her mind daily. How could she be there for everyone? Travis needed her, too, and her responsibilities were becoming out of control. Sometimes the only answer we have is silence in a relationship, so energies in lack or often seen as "ego" and love can shift. She knew she needed to take time to reflect and evaluate what wasn't working in her life, make the necessary changes, and allow herself to process through the grief of her lost friendship and her son's new challenges. So, she chose to face it head on and grow through it all. After the healing occurred slowly in Stephanie and Brandi's relationship, they were able to understand the critical need for them both to take a break. They reviewed the important parts of their friendship, including the crazy fun, the hysterical laughter, the family connections, and the giving qualities that came so naturally to them both. Stephanie has now become a fabulous spokesperson for this challenge, acknowledging powerful truths in her own life and educating others in theirs.

Can you relate to the situation between Stephanie and Brandi? Have you ever had this happen to you in a friendship? The lack of healthy, loving boundaries becomes evident sometimes in our lives. We evolve into becoming an integral part of an individual living their life at the expense of ours. How does this happen? The answer is...very slowly, so that we often don't even notice it. It steals one small piece of us and our energy at a time, until it is too late. We begin the process fully committed, justifying many of our actions as helping, supporting, assisting, and giving. Meanwhile, we deplete our own energy and neglect our self-care, and personal responsibilities. How can we create these boundaries without injuring our own hearts and the hearts of others? We must understand how comfort zones work, when and why they are important, and when they are not. Relationships teach us about ourselves and prompt us to recognize our own challenges and blessings. They bring forth a positive and beautiful energy when the love and inner gifts of each person are shared with one other. When individuals are in "lack," or ego, however, the gifts possessed by each person are not fully seen or appreciated. Both parties can become self-absorbed and see only their own NEEDS. This creates a focus on the needs (lack) and not on the gifts, strengths, and purpose in life.

The Comfort Zone and Grief

Any area of our lives can easily become a comfort zone. Some of my clients walk with me as we work together to help them heal from traumatic events that have resulted in grief, deep anger and frustration, or depression. We begin with acknowledging they are in the comfort zone to gain safety for a time. Friends, family, and colleagues may have told them they should be able to move on by now, and they have not been able to do so on their own. My response to them is, "No one can tell you when being in the zone is *long enough*. Only you can." Providing you are moving forward with healing and adjusting your "steps" in life, you're making progress.

In my previous work with families of children with medically fragile or challenging disorders, I observed the consistent phase of grief they faced. We call it chronic grief, and it continues throughout their lives, regarding the relationship with their child. My act of support was to be present and supportive and to bring out the best moments I could with the parents, siblings, and children. This would include celebrations of small "steps" and milestones, along with therapeutic ways to reach them. If you remember my story of Chelsea and her first steps, being a part of those moments was a great honor. Learning to listen while a parent was angry, tired, fearful, or just frustrated was all a part of my role and relationship with them. I felt privileged and blessed to be a part of their journey, even when it ended in the loss and passing of a child. Please know, I grieved along with them. This became a risk I was willing to take, however, and one that definitely brought me out of my comfort zone. I chose to take that risk because the purpose in it was worth it to me. Love means being there in the comfort zone, the places of pain and grief, as well as, in the steps of success and victory.

Throughout my career, I also worked with youth, for a time, as a counselor and teacher at our church. I remember during one particular event, the minister asked me how my work was going. He was very aware of the work I did and with whom I worked. He also knew it was a path of purpose and passion for me. On this night, however, he asked me a poignant question I was not quite prepared to answer. With all the heartfelt emotion he could share, he posed his question, "Do you grieve?" What did he just say? I was confused. Do I grieve in my job? Why would I grieve? He knew the difficult situations I was sometimes placed in with families and their children. Therefore, the question wasn't out of line at all. It just caught me off guard at that moment, I suppose. I asked myself very quickly, "*Do I grieve?*" Of course, I quickly responded, "No." I was emphatic when I said it and thought I meant it. I went on to share with him how every step with each child was celebrated and, when necessary, our focus would be readjusted on the smallest of moments to see the most gradual shifts.

This is how I worked and why I connected so well with my families. It's also a prominent reason for my becoming such an advocate on the state and national levels and why I became a keynote speaker and facilitator for the importance our work plays in the lives of so many. I never forgot the question posed to me that day, though, and often reflected upon it. *Do I grieve?*

Sometimes when we are in the comfort zone, allowing ourselves to gain healing, nurturing, and insights that will propel us back out into the world again, we do grieve. Sometimes we grieve the loss of what could have been or the reluctant acceptance of what IS and will be. Not that our new reality is wrong; it is just different, and perhaps, not what we had wanted. It's like planning for a trip to Disney and waking up, looking out of the window at your destination, and realizing you aren't in Disney, but Legoland instead. Legoland is a fun place and full of new sights to see, but it's not Disney. You are still on vacation, but it's not Disney. How do you feel? Disappointed, frustrated, or even a little depressed? Sometimes it takes a while to see the beauty of the new, to recognize and appreciate the amazing views of what is yet to come. In other words, it's alright to be in the comfort zone, to take in the new views, to sit with them a while and get adjusted, allowing yourself to feel the shift in mindset toward being happy about the change. Will you still miss what could have been? Possibly. However, you will eventually find your new "normal" in life and embrace it, too.

Developing a Personal "I AM"

I believe the "zone" is a place where we can experience a shifting of our personal "I AM" or authentic self. We need to encounter this at times to bring about transformation and purpose in our lives. If I asked you to positively finish the sentence, "I am_____," using your own thoughts and feelings, what would you say? Would it be any of the following?

> I am a mom.
> I am a daughter.
> I am an entrepreneur.
> I am a fashionista.
> I am a friend.
> I am a caregiver.
> I am a wife, partner, or significant other.
>
> Or would you say?
> I am courageous and strong.
> I am empowered.
> I am honest.
> I am joyful and caring.

I AM's are truly the core of what defines us each day, and whether they are positive or negative only enhances how we feel about ourselves, situations surrounding us, and others we encounter and connect with daily. As you have probably observed, life experiences can shift our "I AM's" and expand our understanding of ourselves and others. My life experiences are no different. They have shifted and redefined my personal "I AM" many times. For example, my own "I AM" began its major shift as my focus narrowed in on personal steps toward health and family. Early in 2010, my own life and work path was drastically detoured with increased caregiving for my mom. As we progressed through the stages of the ever-changing needs her illness presented, the first major shift in my I AM began.

Let's talk about the "I AM NOT's" in life for a moment. They are equally important. During our comfort zone experiences, we learn to strengthen them both as we find our way. Would I want to state my I AM NOT as: *I AM NOT healthy,* or *I AM NOT fully well yet, but I will be?* We can also switch our I AM NOT statements to more positive I AM's, which would sound like this, for example: *I AM working toward living a life of health and wellness and feeling fabulous.* Which statements do you believe activate the mind, body, and spirit to follow a positive direction? Which ones bring more health, abundance, and happiness? What affirmations motivate the pursuit of intention we want each day to choose the following: healthy eating, balancing my day with meditation and work my heart loves, sleeping the hours my body needs, and creating moments of joy and movement I crave so I *can* feel fabulous? For certain, it is *not* "I AM NOT healthy" or "I AM chronically ill." I have worn that label, at times, and the T-shirt that accompanies it. Our I AM's are powerful in creating personal health and wellness in mind, body, and spirit. Knowing our strongest I AM's become the foundation to build our thoughts and actions even more.

Let's dive in deeper into the I AM NOT statements for a moment. These I AM NOT statements provide an inside look at our past and present challenges, seen through the lenses of false statements we have believed and fears we may have developed over the years. They will serve to negatively impact our lives, unless we shift them. It is necessary to adopt a daily intention of redefining the thoughts, beliefs, and actions of the I AM NOT's to be the new confident I AM mantras we take with us as we walk forward in life. Then, these I AM NOT's, once unleashed and shifted, can catapult us into newness.

> These forces of challenge and false beliefs have become what I term, anchors in the ocean floor of our past, effecting our present and placing our future "at risk."

When I work with my individual clients, we always begin with an exercise to stretch their thoughts and connect with their core feelings, memories, and challenges. Finding what empowers them and gives them the ability to move forward is just as important as uncovering what "anchors" them in the steps along their paths. There are fears and lies they believe have created an anchor. The anchored beliefs we carry each day have a long and heavy chain, which allows them to be secured deeply on the ocean floor within each of us. The chain continues to collect debris from our lives and converts it to the barnacles that cling and embed themselves into the heavy links. Each barnacle adheres itself with almost a cement-like feel, withstanding all attempts to be removed. Fears themselves operate just like that in our lives. We start off believing they are meant to help us, to shield us from harm, and to protect us from other thoughts and actions. Instead, our fears trick us into believing we need them. With each step forward, we drag those beliefs with us, collecting all the moments, experiences, and relationships that support and perpetuate that fear in our lives. Let's look at the steps forward and find out how we can begin to recognize the removal of these barnacles and the steps necessary to pull up each of these anchors.

First, what are your I AM's? Can you list ten? Twenty? Thirty? Which ones are roles and responsibilities? Which ones are characteristics and strengths you possess?

Second, define your I AM NOT's. Are any of them related? Is there a common theme you can identify between them?

These themes become our Soul Stories. Our stories are created by both our I AM's and our I AM NOT's to define our purpose and focus on our passions. They are the tapestry of our Soul Stories that connect our hearts in positive and negative ways. The positives become our "heartstrings" to pull on as needed when we want to be reminded of the goodness, love, and blessings in our lives. The negatives may appear as "anchors," which are deeply embedded in our soul with barnacles of experiences adhering themselves to the heavy chain. These anchors are the weights of the fears we may have about life's challenges. They are what maintains the links of the chain as we begin to pursue our dreams and hopes.

It's important to note that as we age, we shift our I AM's in an even greater way. As children, we gained our independence one step at a time. Yet, as we age, we lose our independence in steps, from loss of homes, friends, family members, driving, health, and memories. Even the smallest of steps can seem like giant ones. Looking back, I recall watching my mom struggle as she became more dependent on my husband and me. She lost patience with her situation, not understanding the impact of her thinking and behavior due to her circumstances. I witnessed my mom ultimately become a different person as she transitioned to the last stage of her life. As a result, my role as her daughter became most important, only equal to my ability to manage her health care each day. Nurses, medications, diet, and oxygen were all just pieces of the daily routine, paired with emotional reactions. On a positive note, her faith, love, and sense of humor remained during the four years we were blessed to have her. This awakened the spirit of true sacrifice, trust, and transition in life, for both of us. Mom chose to release her anger and bitterness in exchange for love, while I embraced the lessons of forgiveness and empathy. Her willingness to live in her comfort zone both her biggest challenge and greatest gift. She shared her openness in wanting to know what to expect in the days leading up to her death, while choosing faith over fear, as she took those final steps. Mom also displayed trust in the greatest gift I could offer her, the role of being her daughter. It became a valuable gift to me as well, as our time together developed into memories we would both hold dear. In turn, my own walk was forever changed through this treasured experience. Would I view this new "I AM" as something to which I was shackled? Or would I choose to shine in the radiance and blessing of being a caregiver and a daughter? I chose to shine in the knowing and used it to illuminate my path forward, even though I had no idea where my journey would lead me next. In fact, I realized later, this season and experience brought the preparation I needed for my own next steps along the journey.

> Yes, grief is dark when you enter, but hope in life is the light.

The Truth Behind Dis-ease

Over the years, I have learned a primary truth about disease. *Dis-ease* is a neglecting of ourselves, a losing of our balance in life; yet, it tends to create a season of listening and learning to be still and thrive. As quickly as I could return to working around the country, I did. I believe now it was to assist in my grieving process as I was continuing to heal emotionally. See, from my perspective, at least I knew who I was as a speaker, coach, consultant, and author. It wasn't something I wrestled with or had to redefine at that moment in time. These responsibilities also come along with a feeling of natural stride and pure, comfortable motion. I could perform them with ease as they came naturally. I needed this period of reprieve to find my cadence and rhythm in life again. What I found instead, however, was a different outcome entirely. This time, walking in what would have been my comfort zone felt like putting on my favorite shoes that were now two sizes too small. My old life and career didn't fit me anymore. My "I AM" was different, and the calling and mission had shifted. It was at this time, after only four months back on the road, my path came to an abrupt halt again.

I had been working across the country speaking about the effectiveness of a positive mindset and how to shift thoughts and practice in our work and life. My itinerary was a strategy nightmare, and each day I was driving, flying, or speaking somewhere different. I woke up one morning to realize I only had a few days left of this crazy schedule. I couldn't wait! By the weekend, I would be flying home to be with my family, or so I thought. Instead, I would be thrust back into the "comfort zone" experience after a series of events. This one would be more than just one of life's "wake-up" calls.

I dressed for work and packed my bags for yet another long drive. I knew as I placed my items in the rental car that this would be my final day of excessive schedules. I only needed to facilitate an eight-hour training, which I thought would be no problem. I had done this many times before and, by now, was a master at it. I would be driving between two locations, eating whatever fast food or gas station cuisine I could find along the way, while trying to navigate my new surroundings. Winding roads, bad food, foggy weather, and intense rain would all be just part of the journey that day. When I did have cell coverage, I could make calls to the office and speak with my assistant. She was masterful at supporting me in my work. She knew my clients all over the country, and they trusted her decisions on what needed to be done. She was my voice when I had to be using mine each day for facilitating, coaching, and leading. That evening, after finding my hotel late into the night, I knew I would collapse on the bed with my body aching from pure exhaustion. Still, I would push through and finish strong, knowing this was the final leg of the race.

The final few days of speaking engagements began. However, during a particularly long and grueling drive in between event locations, a major storm system had moved in, making the dark, winding roads more ominous. The rain was so heavy in some areas, it left main roads partially under water, which created an unexpected detour, making my already extensive drive three hours longer. When I finally reached my hotel, there were no restaurants open in the small town. Even the grocery store was closed due to weather. I checked into the small hotel and carried my bags to the room. There was a little marketplace in the lobby with very little I could eat, due to my dietary restrictions. I found an apple and some peanut butter, realizing that would have to suffice. As I completed my "meal," while lying on the bed watching an old movie, I felt the numbness and dull aching throughout every inch of me. My head was throbbing, as well, following in tune with the other cries of my depleted body. I fell asleep, fully clothed, only to wake up to a resounding alarm four hours later. Could I do this again? Could I get up, take a shower, pack up and be the dynamic inspirational speaker and facilitator this group needed? After all, it was just one more time, right?

So, I managed to get myself moving forward and focused on the fact that, after today, I would finally be heading home. Yes, I would miss the wonderful people I had the pleasure to meet and interact with. I really had enjoyed the beautiful part of the country I had been blessed to see and experience. Truly, I would never forget the memories made and the lessons these four months had taught me. Still, I missed my family, and it was time to go home. I finished my day of work and drove to the airport hotel, where I settled in with a simple, healthy dinner in bed. As I fell asleep, my thoughts rested on the time I would now have to catch up with my life and focus on other aspects of the business. Little did I know, something different was on the horizon.

The next morning, I woke up with the intense, throbbing pain that only a massive migraine could give. The increased stress, unhealthy eating, dehydration, and intensity of these days all played a role. I called my assistant and asked her to cancel my flight. I was in so much pain it forced me to accept that I wasn't going anywhere. I spent the next two days asleep in my hotel room, with a wonderful front desk staff who brought me hot tea and chicken broth to keep me nourished in between sleeping binges. Eventually, I became confident I could handle the residual effects of the migraine and made my way to the airport for a flight home. My husband picked me up, so glad to have me home again. He took one look at me, though, and knew there would be no celebrating that night. He drove me home and put me back in bed. My body had finally shut down from the schedule and the stress I had placed it under. A few days later, I came out of my comfort zone "slumber" and started to rethink life. My business was changing, and the prospect of being gone for so long didn't even seem interesting anymore. Plus, strangely enough, I still didn't feel very well, and I concluded that it may be time to take care of myself a little bit more.

A few weeks after coming home and having experienced my own personal wake-up call, I still wasn't feeling well. The pain and inflammation had only increased. The fatigue was not relieved by any amount of rest, and the headaches persisted, despite pain relief medication. I had also developed severe pain in the joints of my right hand. One day, I woke up with pain, yet again, but this time it was accompanied by generalized weakness. As a result, I set up an urgent appointment with my primary care physician. Dr. Cunningham is an amazing doctor and had known me for many years. We met for the first time when she had just moved to our area, opened her practice as a new physician, and agreed to take on my mom as her patient. Dr. C was wonderful with my mom and was constantly supporting her until she passed away. She was the first person I called about any concern regarding Mom, and after Mom's passing, I asked her to become my own doctor. I loved her bedside manner, her eagerness to solve a health challenge, and her willingness to network with other amazing specialists who could help with specific health concerns. When I walked into Dr. C's office, she could not believe what poor health I was in or the severe condition of my swollen hand and joints along with extreme pain and fatigue. Years ago, I had been diagnosed with lupus but had never been treated appropriately. She decided to run extensive blood tests and X-rays to see what results we would find and need to treat moving forward. The tests concluded that I was struggling with a new diagnosis, one of rheumatoid arthritis (RA). RA is an autoimmune disease that creates an increased level of inflammation and attacks all the joints in the body. Additional tests showed other medical challenges, and the need for a new rheumatologist was inevitable.

I was in shock! The diagnosis of RA was only the beginning of the journey. I would need to take steps to restore my health, which would include taking new drugs and making lifestyle changes. After three months of my body fighting against itself, I was placed on rounds of biogenic drugs, chemotherapy injections, and pain medications. For the next year, I learned to live a very different life. Some days the pain became great and the exhaustion so intense that staying awake was only possible for a few hours. Trying to take a bath became a major undertaking. The energy to balance and hold my feet steady while stepping in and out of that warm water was exhausting, no matter how therapeutic the bath felt! My work level switched to minimal, and I was reduced to simply coaching clients around the country from the safety and rest of my own home. Traveling, speaking, and meeting with new or prospective clients had come to a halt.

I had to face the realization that healing myself was the first and only goal in my life at that moment. Work could be placed on pause. This shoe-loving woman had been reduced to pajamas and slippers. I began living day to day in what became my comfort zone of life. After being in such a vital position in my work assisting others with their challenges while finding positive aspects of any situation, I walked into a path of utter "lack." A lack of strength, direction, and answers to an illness that seemed to elude many, now appeared to mark my daily life. Each day rolled into the next, and I found myself at a place where nothing felt good. Most days there were more questions than answers.

Finding solace on the couch became my daily ritual. Yes, it was my comfort zone. This couch was in the center of our home, near the kitchen, bathroom and bedroom, providing a front row seat to the swaying trees and hand-crafted deck outside the large windows. My husband had positioned this couch carefully within listening distance, just in case I needed his help. My dear husband was there for it all, even though some days I knew he wondered what the outcome would be in all of this. As a pilot, he travels a great deal and is usually gone for three to four days at a time. So, he worried about me during the days he was away. However, he really put forth the effort to take care of my needs, even during his absence. For example, in preparation for leaving me alone for a few days, he would cook batches of healthy comfort food, usually soups, and put them in thermoses for me to access them better while he was gone. He would set me up on the couch with bottles of water and hot tea, offering plenty of cuddles before he left. Can you imagine walking away from your ailing wife while she was alone and not truly able to fend for herself?

His heart was heavy, and his responsibility to me was great. Yet, he willingly took it on with strength and compassion. Fortunately, we had a few close neighbors who were just a call away when I needed help or if something went wrong, requiring an ER visit, which happened frequently. I remember several occasions when my husband landed from a flight and drove straight to the hospital to meet me. Through it all, I learned to be in a spirit of calm and rely on my quiet times, knowing that God held me safely in His hand and walked every step of it with me. I did ask myself a few times, "Will this forever be my life now?" God was the only one who knew the answer, and at that time, He hadn't shared it with me yet. It was a deep time of reflection, prayer, and stillness.

On April 6, 2007, Arianna Huffington, influential author and cofounder and president of the *Huffington Post*, woke up to find herself on the floor in a pool of blood. This event served as her personal wake-up call. After extensive testing and a host of questions left unanswered, she concluded that she needed changes in her life. At the height of her career, she was "thriving," or so it appeared. Suddenly one day, however, it all came to a screeching halt.

When we ignore the signs creeping in all around us, we can slowly miss the little ones, until we are finally stopped full force by one that takes us to our knees. When was the last time you had a good night's rest? What about a full day of nutritional food and drink? Can you find a few minutes of quiet, stillness, meditation time, or prayer in your daily routine? Do you regularly enjoy free time to pursue a fun activity by yourself or with family or friends? If you answered "no" to any or all of these questions, you, too, could find yourself in a comfort zone crash.

I found Arianna's book, *Thrive: The Third Metric to Redefining Success and Creating a Life of Well-being, Wisdom, and Wonder,* incredibly enlightening. It affirmed my glimmer of hope and fueled my faith for the possibility of finding balance and purpose in life again. Going from a place of overwhelming "dis-ease" to standing up and taking one step at a time, was a process of endurance, faith, and hope. At one point, my comfort zone experience felt like it was going to be permanent and I couldn't understand why I had been given a passion in my heart and I wasn't going to be able to pursue it. After finding the right physicians, specialists, and alternative medicine measures, a new journey began for me. This road would be one of increased health and healing, which would continue for the rest of my life. Gaining strength was my new goal. One step at a time, I began re-envisioning my life and my work.

Lessons Learned in the Comfort Zone

What did I learn from my comfort zone experiences? The answer to that is…so much! However, if I had to summarize, I would say: courageously surrender to your journey and magnificence will be born, as you honor the times in your life of both tragedy and triumph. When we are transforming, we do have times in the comfort zone, which can become the best moments of vibrancy we experience. When we quiet our thoughts and listen carefully to the quiet stillness of our own breath and God's wisdom and reassurance, we feel utter peace…even when facing terrible pain. I learned to meditate so deeply that my own heart rate would slow its pace to withstand the pain my body was enduring. Being at peace and resting throughout the day provided me the moments of clarity and reflection on life I was needing. Friedrich Nietzsche beautifully acknowledges, "A man that has a WHY to live can bear any HOW." Learning to hear your "why" in life creates a completely different appreciation and perspective on living in the comfort zone. It is only a moment to "be still and know." What are you facing where *be still and know* is the key?

As I was beginning to understand my newfound steps in life, I was offered a special opportunity with a women's organization based in Los Angeles, BraveHeart Women International. They were expanding their outreach and were looking for some power bloggers who would be willing to write for their online platform with at least a one-year commitment and an article a month. I interviewed and was accepted as one of the bloggers. The honor came with a complimentary invitation to attend a five-day women's conference. I couldn't wait! I felt in my heart that this was to bring forth a shift for me! I would leave that spiritual retreat, spent with other women around the world, and never be the same. Many of my close friends today came from this special event. It awakened my spirit and gave me new insights, as a joy for studying again was rekindled. Thought-provoking leaders such as, Maya Angelou, Jamie Lee Curtis, Valerie Harper, Michael Beckwith, Marianne Williamson, and many others delivered powerful messages that transcended all areas in life and gave us each healing and hope. I also learned that week I still held a need for sisters. Growing up and into adulthood, my sister and I were best friends. We even had careers in a complimentary field. While I was in my doctorate program, she suddenly passed away from a brain aneurysm. With my dad and sister both gone, I became even more of my mom's foundation and emotional security in life. I lost my feeling of being a little sister and grew up very fast. It wasn't until I was in a double circle of hundreds of women hugging and honoring each other that I heard God say, "Here are your sisters, embrace them." It was truly a healing moment for me! That impactful moment ignited a new passion inside of me and became one of the main reasons I wanted to start focusing on the healing and empowerment of women. I had found my "why," my "call to action," and my path of newfound purpose was unleashed!

As we grow, we blossom and bring forth the essence of what we are "BE"-coming. While we are in the comfort zone, we focus more on healing and loving ourselves. You must be in self-love and self-trust to effectively move forward in abundance in your life. Women are feeling individuals. We speak in emotions, and if those emotions are ones of hurt, fear, and ego, others will hear those words resonate in our language, as well as our facial expressions and actions. If the emotions we are feeling are joy, compassion, hope, and love, those are the words of comfort we will be share. When we are in "fight-flight-flee" mode, which usually occurs in moments that activate fear, rejection, hurt, or abandonment, we activate an area of our brain that unleashes adrenaline. It is quick to act, quick to respond, and quick to be on the attack. There are no emotions present in the adrenaline flow, except an autonomic response to threat and competition. Positive relationships are not connected to this response. Relationships are enhanced through positive connectedness and sharing energy that stems from joy, love, gratefulness, and happiness.

My relationship continues with BraveHeart Women International and the community of sisters I have made there. These dedicated and powerful women believe we are led by our hearts and souls and that the leadership found within us changes our families, communities, and countries. As women are rising, we are coming together with personal and global purpose. Our collaboration is essential. Being authentic in our work as women requires passion, connection, innovation, and creativity. We work with groups of women, empowering them to become more connected in their lives and work, rather than simply focusing on the "ladder" of success.

The Stress is Real

The stress we face in the struggle is quite real. This dis-ease has been deeply rooted by the words and actions of others, as well as, situations outside of our control. As the daily caregiver to my beautiful mom, even though I acknowledged it was a gift of love for both of us, I certainly felt the source of challenge in it, too. We were both giving up familiar consistencies and expectations to find the new normal in everyday routines and experiences. Her independent days were gone, and we all knew life was changing forever.

The chronic stress that we endure in our challenges causes us to revert to ways of reacting that may not be at our highest level of critical thinking and problem solving. We call it "downshifting" into the fight-flight-flee processes. This activation, at high frequency, will overload the brain with hormones and begin a long process of mind-body connections. Let's briefly walk through an example of this stress-induced journey together. A challenge occurs. It can be a sudden, life-altering event or the gradual build up and overload of the constant stresses occurring in daily life. It is in these moments that everything you are experiencing becomes a "threat," resulting in a chain reaction of events within the body as it stands at high alert to protect your personal safety.

When you are in this active state of alert from intense, ongoing stress, whether it is self-induced or real, you are completely committed and involved! The longer you stay in this overload or "fight-flight-flee" state of being, the rigidity and resistance in your operating systems can occur. This often leads to the developing of more barnacles on the anchors in your life. When you shift your responses away from chaos and calamity toward relaxation and resolution, you possess the ability to respond with your whole mind, body, and spirt.

For example, we can diffuse the active flow of negative bodily responses to stress with a process interrupter. One illustration of a process interrupter through positive bonds we develop with others. Close physical contact and emotional connection can trigger my favorite hormone, sometimes called "The Cuddle Hormone," oxytocin. Oxytocin is also known as the "happiness" hormone, especially in women. It assists us in feelings of being safe and secure, even when our reactions may have told us differently.

One of my mentors, Dr. Ellie Drake, founder of BraveHeart Women International Community, discusses this concept of oxytocin release as a way to stay in mind-body-spirit alignment and to create the breath which is necessary. When you can easily learn to release the hormone during your daily routines, your body will learn to find its own flow and nurture itself. It is a cleansing breath of "in through the nose and out through the mouth" with a strong, deep "HHAAAAH" sound as you let it all the way out. It will resonate through your diaphragm and you will even feel it in your throat, as it involves the whole body in its release.

The Real Housewives of Dallas' Cary Deuber connected with me at the recommendation of her "housewife" friend and co-star, Stephanie Hollman. Cary and I connected and started her journey to finding her balance in life and work. Cary had some unique situations, trying to coordinate all of life's components, which for her were very diverse and sometimes disjointed. She was focused on maintaining her need for alignment and spiritual practice in her yoga, meditation, and heathy living. Her family life includes being a mom to a preschool-aged daughter and two step children, who are high priorities to her. Add in her career with husband, Mark, in a very active and demanding plastic surgery clinic, where she is a surgical nurse responsible for patients of her own during consultations and injections. Keeping the practice running smoothly, with continued growth, is a key goal for both of them. Cary continues to be a cast member on RHOD, so filming, appearances, promotions, endorsements, and managing her additional more public career, has already become a full-time job. They are also a very active couple in the community of Dallas, as many of the "housewives" are. They both sponsor, attend, and chair a large quantity of the fundraising and philanthropic work in the area. They share a passion of traveling extensively and entertaining, especially since Mark is a fabulous chef. Are you beginning to see the picture? Balance...what balance? How was she to decide which responsibilities and roles to decrease or place ahead of the others? We had to begin with what her beliefs were in regard to balance and what would that look like in her life and the lives of her family. We then focused on how to shift her belief in what was most important and prioritize that consistently.

Do you ever feel like Cary? I know I do! Learning how to create balance begins with our beliefs and where the roots of their assumptions and aspirations lie. So, what happened with Cary? If you haven't seen Season 2, you may want to watch a few episodes. She struggled for a while, but her and Mark were able to release her from a few days at work to be with their daughter, Zuri. Being a mom was such a fulfilling joy for her! When we find the balance AND the bliss in life, the frustration and struggle fades.

I AM...ENOUGH

Belief is embedded deeply within us when it comes to what we value and see in life. Some of us have heard messages of support, love, beauty, and encouragement in our lives. Yet, there are others who have been told lies or misconceptions disguised as truth. So, we accepted them as truth and adopted them into our own personal belief systems about ourselves and how life works.

A close friend, Julia, once elaborated on a story about her family. We were each sharing about family legacy and the power behind the words our mothers and grandmothers spoke over us. She had been told by the women in her family that it was easier to move forward in life if you don't put forth too much effort. This way, it would make the disappointments easier. She was also instructed, even as a young adolescent, not to make big decisions or goals in life, because it was not worth the struggle. Thank goodness she didn't believe this herself, nor did she make it a part of her operating system in life. Comfort zones can be dangerous if they ARE the norm and not valued. The favorite quote she shared, which defined her challenge as she broke free of this generational belief system was, "Caution: this emotion or reaction may produce joy." Julia was told repeatedly, "Don't get too excited or you may be destined for a life of defeat." Wow, again, I'm so grateful that she released the fear and the emotions embedded within them, so she could actively receive the bounty of joy that was just within her grasp every day.

It is easier for us to accept limiting beliefs as they provide a safety or comfort zone reaction for us. Learning to walk in strength without judgement, shame, or control is key. Brene Brown experienced an extreme example of this. Her work on shame is a foundation for all of us to stand on and realize we are ENOUGH. We can dare greatly in our lives knowing this one phrase and placing it deeply in our soul as it blossoms, I AM ENOUGH.

Creating moments to capture and give us foundation to the belief that I AM ENOUGH comes with recreating snapshots in your life to look different and more supportive of a better life. We want to focus in on the memories that fill us up, not remove our joy. When we are struggling with our limiting beliefs, we are unable to move forward in life. Everything overwhelms us; we fall back into the comfort zone of what nurtures us and what anchors us to our prior operating system. Yes, change is difficult, but so worth the struggle to hold on and move forward in life where abundance, love, and joy reside.

As Stephanie has shared, she has faced her own struggles with depression by being overwhelmed by expectations, family, outreach, and even friendships. I've always told her hashtag in life should be #realwoman24/7. We are real women with real hearts and real needs. We also need to be lifting each other up in honor, not in competition, drama, gossip, and lies.

What are you bound to in your life? What are your slippers in the comfort zone? Are you willing to shift your thinking, interactions, goals, diet, and more to see and feel a new life? What if it means changing your friends, your work, your location, your relationships, and your "I AM?" Are you willing to see your current "I AM" and own it?

These authentic and empowering "I AM" statements are driven by our relationships in life and work. Many of my clients share their stories of "stepping out" of challenging relationships with significant others, family members, and even friendships. The theme of boundaries in these relationships is key and usually at the core of the challenge. One of my favorite experts in this field is Dr. Henry Cloud. His book *Necessary Endings* is a wonderful resource in these situations where toxic people in our lives need to be removed. He wrote, "In your business and perhaps your life, the tomorrow that you desire and envision may never come to pass if you do not end some things you are doing today. In it you will see that endings are a natural part of the universe, and your life and business must face them, stagnate, or die." Dr. Cloud so eloquently states our joint belief, "the good cannot begin until the bad ends."

I will discuss these boundaries and endings further in the next few chapters where we focus on "stepping up" and "stepping forward," as well as leaping with vision. Yes, we have to step OUT to find our newest and bravest I AM's. Even with the I AM's and their power, the I AM NOT's push us and strengthen our conviction even further. When we don't acknowledge the voices we have heard in our lives for so many years, we accept them as our own…we begin to hear the negative statements in our own voice instead of those who originally said them to us. It is time to claim your identity and true self for yourself! What are some of the things you have heard in your life? Do you believe you are that person?

Comfort zone experiences are there for a season or a moment in our lives. They give us the soft place to fall, the blanket to wrap up in, or the covers to pull over our head. Healing when it assists us in the transition to something greater, something new, something more brilliant and breathtaking in life where the old "I AM's" don't define us any longer.

These are "be still" moments for us. I believe it is in times that we can rest and gain the support of our highest power, God. The scripture in Psalms 46:10 reads, "Be still and know that I am God." He is there for us to rest in the pure "knowing." It is in these opportunities of stillness and quiet that we grow the most in order to GLOW brighter and illumine our path forward.

I have always been able to keep a high level pace and manage multiple things at one time. One of my close friends in faith once said to me, "Lori, God does say to lie down in green pastures and be still every once in a while just as much as he wants us running His race." At that moment I heard her words and realized their impact in my life. Maybe it was time for a change, one of more balance and moments of bliss. Some of the work I read around the concepts of balance and bliss suggest it is unattainable and therefore not something we should focus on. Can we achieve balance and bliss in our lives?

Through my weeks and sometimes now days of healing, I have focused more on "being" to bring back the balance in my life filled with "doing" actions and implementing our calling. In the comfort zone, it is our time for "being," our moment to learn, reflect, and create a new, more insightful self. Then, we are ready to take action with the excitement our new focus has provided us. It is a call we receive for activation each time with higher and higher steps UP to create the greatest impact in our lives and those of others.

For me to experience even more, I must use the comfort zone as a neutral space for a moment of comfort and healing. I work with my clients on defining what this means for them and when to know it is time to step OUT once again. Yes, sometimes leaving it means higher risk and anxiety, which can be a moment of stumbling as you gain traction. Yet, when you are in this level of action forward you will:

1. Be more productive and push self-induced boundaries.
2. Be better at dealing with new and unexpected change. Researcher and professor Brene Brown explains, "the worst thing we can do is pretend fear and uncertainty don't exist." Take controlled risks and manageable steps as you step OUT onto this new ground.
3. Be ready to push your own boundaries as you start moving forward.
4. Be creative and brainstorm possibilities for solutions. Stay focused on what is working, rather than what isn't working.
5. Let life inspire you! Look for ways to celebrate your new forward movement and when challenges do arise, breathe and leap over them with appreciation.

One of the most difficult steps we take in our life is out of the comfort zone. Even though it can be filled with pain, loss, transition, deep memories, chronic "dis-ease," sometimes the fear of moving is heavier than the desire to grasp the blessings and abundance offered to us. This is what keeps us anchored in our experiences. Even as I wrote this chapter, I knew it would be the most challenging for me to share. Why? It is in our own vulnerability that we are at our most authentic and most real self. We may not like who "she" is and avoid her in the mirror each morning when she shows up. It is so much easier to live where we are constantly in action, not in stillness. Yet, where we do our best growth is in reflection, in the quiet moments when God speaks to us loudly in all of the things surrounding us. It is where we return to again and again to feel His presence, curl up in His lap, have Him listen to our stories, and just breathe in the goodness of being at peace. When we are ready to step out, we ask for the path to present itself to us so we can move forward in our next exciting stage of life's adventure. Our comfort zone is a place to find temporary solace, ask and receive answers, and to remind ourselves who we really are and how amazing we are becoming.

At one time in my traveling and coaching work, I was blessed to be bringing a specialized curriculum in shifting mindset and growing your strengths with a large group of youth in an alternative program as they were completing a school-based credit-recovery program in hopes of finishing their high school diploma. Their counselors, therapists, and teachers were with us as we engaged in a high-level experience with the students. It is important to know these youth people, ages sixteen to eighteen, were desperately trying to walk away from drugs or other addictions, dealing drugs, being a member of a gang, overcoming a legacy of family poverty and illiteracy, abuse, domestic violence, living on the streets or in their cars, and having children of their own as well as outside jobs to support themselves. We were on the border of Mexico and the influence of challenges with their families still over the border or other situations as I shared above was overwhelming for many of them. The personnel that supported them were some of the most caring and dedicated I have met. Their heartfelt mission was to give these youth a new start in a brand new life.

Sometimes a slight push is necessary when we have been in our comfort zone shelter for a while. We've been talking about being our authentic and true selves in different ways. This is another chance to be different and it may be an even greater step toward creating a new self than any other. Being what I call your most "outrageous self" can be eye-opening and a way to free new or dormant feelings and engage a shift toward truly stepping out.

Trying new things can make you ready to step OUT of your comfort zone. Just like children, we are natural risk-takers. As we get older, we lose some of our ability to step OUT and experience things which could cause of failure or even in some cases, success.

As you step out of your comfort zone to be your newest self, you are feeling and hearing a CALL, a call to action. It is saying, "this is YOUR time, grasp the opportunity." Calling yourself to action means being proactive, using your gifts and assets to assist others and yourself, and meeting the growing needs you may find in your life. We create a call to action with three steps:

1. Engage in your "why." What is your "why" for stepping OUT at this time? Sometimes as I share, you may be dedicating your "why" to someone until you own the call for yourself.
2. Create a vision board or a vision page in your journal for taking this step. Fill it with positive statements, words, and pictures to visually support you in your steps.
3. Fuel your fire with stimulating ideas, explorations, and small successes you will look for in your new path.

When I was working with a talented group of youth using the psychology of Asset-Based Thinking, which I will share more about later, I met a wonderful young lady who attended a local middle school. Her name was Elizabeth and I want to share her story in hope you will feel the impact of the comfort zone shift through her own personal call to action.

December 1, 2008, I experienced a terrible break in my foot during my favorite dance class. This was a devastating blow, for dancing was my life. I was put in a cast for three and half months followed by three months of rehab. At first, I was angry with the world, and couldn't understand the purpose of my "unfortunate" fate. My mom helped me through each day and reminded me that I was always able to find the silver lining in each situation I encountered, and this one should be no different. Therefore, I decided to focus even harder on my academics. I received several awards as a result of my new focus, and in the end, was selected to be a Student Ambassador through the People to People Ambassador Program to travel through Europe.

This program was developed on the belief that "direct interaction between ordinary citizens around the world can promote cultural understanding and world peace." This philosophy caught my eye, as I have always believed that peace is the best option. It's a small world, and people need to realize they are very much the same and if they would get to know one another, they would see the similarities which could lead to peaceful relationships and helping of one another.

In order to have the opportunity to make a difference, I had to raise money to fund the trip. I decided to make and sell bottle cap magnets for lockers, refrigerators, and necklaces. I had to **think BIG** to try to meet my goal, so I went to several shops asking if they would sell my product. After many "No's" I finally got a **"Yes!"** I am also able to sell them weekly at my middle school, (thanks to my principal) and my elementary school. I have sold them at a dance convention and a dance studio, and made special necklaces for my dentist, utilizing his logo, for use in consoling patients who had a "rough" visit. Then to top it all, I have the pleasure of working with ABT!

The process towards realizing my dream has been as much of a journey as traveling Europe will be. I have learned so much, and will have the chance to help so many, as a result of my "unfortunate" fate. Through this winding road of incredible events I have kept a positive mind-set that has helped me along. I carry with me my motto: **There is a reason for everything, though you may not see it, and there is a rainbow at the end of every storm.** Taking a positive approach leads to a better, happier, outcome. I count my blessings every day, and I can only hope that every teen will choose to do so as well.

The rest of the story is that Elizabeth was nominated Student Ambassador of the Year for 2010 and won! She is now speaking out to teens in assemblies and keynotes to share her story in hopes of inspiring them to find their personal call to action.

Life is too short to not collect each moment, each blessing, and each breath as we are standing still or moving forward. Now it is time to step OUT of your comfort zone and really live as you honor where you have been! Remember, it is here for you to return when great growth is necessary or when transformation is happening. Our steps are a cycle in life, each with their own beauty and purpose, just like YOU.

I love this poem by Pam Reinke, called "Boldly Be."

> *Whatever is in you to be,*
> *Whoever you love is your fire.*
> *Ignite it, trust it, it is a gift born of your spirit.*
> *Be it in words, dance, colors, or a song...have absolute faith in what you have been given.*
> *Chase it no matter how elusive, be it...however challenging, pursue it without pause, seek to...*
> *Boldly be whatever is in your heart to be.*

It is your time. Step OUT of your comfort zone...**Be brave, be bold, be YOU!**

Walk with Lori: Comfort Zone

One of the first sessions I conduct with my clients is "Your Own I AM's." If you were to complete the statement, "I am _____" ten times, what would the results be? Do you embrace and "own" them or are they things others tell us? How difficult was this activity?

What are those comfort zone moments for you? Describe a recent one and what occurred to result in being in the zone.

Why do you feel...describe the feelings associated with being in the zone for you.

Have you ever stayed in the comfort zone for too long, according to your family, friends, colleagues, or others?

Your brilliance comes from seeing who you REALLY are & bringing HER with you.

~Lori Dixon~

chapter four
Step UP: Walking One Step at a Time

"We are not a lake, but a river which flows."
—Ellie Drake, BraveHeart Women

Iyanla Vanzant uses the phrase, "in the meantime" in her work to finding yourself and the love you want. Isn't that perfect? "In the meantime" doesn't mean the comfort zone and it doesn't mean I'm now fully engaged and rocking life. It means, "I'm starting to walk OUT and step UP just a little more, as I am figuring out this new road in my journey."

How about you? Can you relate? For me, "stepping up" consists of a few major concepts and strategies. It all begins with an understanding of those pivotal moments in life, what experiences have occurred to shift you or catapult you out of the comfort zone. Once we are launched into action, we continue our journey with the *Illumination Insights*: (1) igniting the process of intentions, (2) embracing the aspects of change, and (3) creating confidence and courage. To assist us when struggle appears, we will need further tools that I call *Simplicity Signals*.

Stepping UP all starts with pivotal moments. Stories are powerful and connect us with experiences in our own lives as we learn about another person's journey. I'd like to share a story with you about slippers, not the well-known "ruby slippers," nor Cinderella's "glass slippers," but my very own pair, the Sapphire Slippers.

The Story of the Sapphire Slippers

I do love shoes and as you read, in my comfort zone I was only wearing slippers and flip flops. Now as a beach girl, I love my flip flops and sandals, but for business they just don't work as well with a suit or dress, especially in Texas.

As I began stepping out of my comfort zone, I embraced my newly found purpose of supporting others who were walking through their own life challenges. I wanted to start finding new things to wear and step up into some new work and ideas. One of my friends, Melissa, was an owner of a high-end designer boutique where she also sold consignment items. I loved fashion and always enjoyed shopping with and for others, as well as finding a fabulous deal wherever I went. It is kind of a game to find the "holy grail" of fashion, don't you think? Gifts from my sweet friend always included clothing that looked fabulous on me, without the lofty price tag, since my ever-changing physical appearance was a factor. Having beautiful and fun pieces pulled for me made me feel special! Since I was also starting to lose weight due to the new nutritional protocol I was following, she helped with my wardrobe needs while paying attention to my budget. We both knew I wouldn't be wearing the items very long with my frequently fluctuating sizes. The consignment part of the shop gave me a wonderful way to sell back the clothing and use the profit to purchase new items. This is where my favorite phrase of "bless…bless" began, which I will share a little more of the meaning with you later in the book.

In between "retail therapy" moments, Melissa and I would share our gifts with each other. Melissa would listen and support me in ideas of business, marketing, and of course, fashion. I would also give her coaching in a positive environment and practice my spiritual gift of visionary intuitive insights. Melissa always had a way of finding just the right thing for me, helping me to take one more step in my fashion evolution journey. Remember, I had been wearing slippers and flats for the duration of my illness and even though heels had always been a part of my daily attire, I could no longer fit them on my inflamed feet. For Christmas, Melissa and her assistant, Trey, found a beautiful pair of sapphire blue high-heel pumps by Stuart Weitzman, who was one of my favorite designers. They creatively packaged them in a fun way, waiting for me to unwrap the unassuming box, wondering what was inside. Of course, I squealed happily at the first sight of their shiny leather uppers, pointed toes, and perfect little two-inch heels for me to begin walking in again. We lovingly called them my sapphire slippers, inspired by the infamous ruby slippers from *The Wizard of Oz*. What a wonderful support group of friends had come into my life just when I needed them! My sapphire slippers became a symbol of my new journey and stepping UP into a new life.

The newest Cinderella movie contains the inspiring quote that serves as a beautiful example of how I felt in this moment. "This is perhaps one of the greatest risks any of us will take, to be seen as we truly are." Cinderella realizes the importance of looking forward in life, rather than focusing on what she had lost, as she began to embrace her personal intention, "not who I was, but who I am now" in all she envisioned ahead. I realized the same. My "I AM" had shifted and these new sapphire shoes were just a small piece of the evolution of a new life emerging. How did this happen? What did I put into place to shift my perspective and envision the future? Well, to heal involves risk, and to begin to risk again, I needed glimpses of hope.

For three months, I stepped up into my previous skills and talents. My focus became using them to assist others in their business outreach and even with families in need of caregiving and medical networking. It made me feel engaged in life again.

Supporting others, coaching, consulting, and walking with each person along the way was my first visible evidence of my ability to work again. I remained involved with both worlds in attempt to "try on" the possibilities of what was to come next on my new path. Speaking on the road, coaching and consulting with long days and high stress, would no longer be the place for me. I would miss the relationships I forged, but I knew my path in life had taken a different turn. Being near home in the Dallas-Fort Worth area seemed much more conducive to this new journey. The ability to drive to a client, work, and drive home, to eat and sleep in my own bed, was refreshing and much more in alignment with my need for balance and maintaining my health.

As I continued to step up into finding my "sweet spot" in life and work again, my dreams and visions began to take on the appearance of a reality. The more I learned about myself, the more challenges became only a memory and fueled the drive to keep going. My plan had developed a focus. *I wanted to help other women.* Would it be to assist those who were experiencing chronic health issues, as well as other insurmountable challenges? I wasn't exactly certain of the scope of life challenges I would be assisting with or how it would all come together. I did, however, know how to start walking forward. Sometimes that's where it starts. We may not have everything figured out before we start the journey. That's okay. Sometimes all that's needed to reach a destination is a tank full of gas, a reliable car, and the will to press the gas pedal and drive.

ILLUMINATON INSIGHT: Igniting Powerful Intentions

Envisioning a life forward gives us hope and a newfound view of opportunities that await us. Realizing we are co-creators in life allows us to set or ignite intention with one step at a time. Our intentions can illumine our path forward with such purpose, like a flashlight that casts its beautiful glow in the dark just when we need it. When we can plan for those moments of walking in faith on a path full of triumphs and tragedies, the path just ahead becomes clearer. We then become better prepared for the lessons it will bring.

When Stephanie and Cary chose to be involved with *The Real Housewives of Dallas*, they deeply thought through this decision, involving both families and friends. The question they faced was, "Should I step UP into this journey?" They would be opening their lives to a platform which can be revealing sometimes and may even spotlight the negative aspects of relationships. They both knew it was not a choice to be made lightly. Each season it is the same for the entire cast. *Do I open up more of my life again? Can I personally handle the intense work, insane schedule, and fast pace of filming and appearances, while remaining healthy in the pursuit? How does this affect my family and my children?* We think fame and the limelight is glamorous, imagining we would all want it if we had the choice. The truth is, it is full of both challenges *and* joys, just like any job. Each of the "housewives" and I spent hours talking about igniting their intentions for another season, along with the purpose and focus for the current season they were filming. We also discussed how they were creating balance between working, community outreach, and family. As a result, it was evident they needed to make very committed choices and stay focused, while life around them was unfolding.

You may ask yourself similar questions before igniting the intentions you so desire in your life. Can you personally embrace and step forward into this new opportunity or challenge? Will your friends and family support you? Who or what would create a hurdle in your endeavor and why?

For me, it became clear that it was time to step up again. My comfort zone didn't fit me anymore, and I was ready to begin walking with others again. Teaching, sharing, and facilitating the knowledge and experience God gifted me with was a new purpose and passion of mine. Bringing with me what I had learned would serve as part of my new calling...I could feel it in my heart. It was time to create a workshop on how to envision the next steps when life takes an unexpected turn. This described the very thing I, myself, was living through, walking just a few steps ahead in the process. I had coached and supported numerous others in my career, yet seeing it unfold in my own life was even more powerful. My moments of "being" were finally becoming moments of "doing." My innate gifts of being a visionary were activated and came peeking through my work. I wasn't quite ready to reveal *how* I received God's direction on the feelings of others, where they needed the support, and how to walk with them as they found their answers. The opportunity to do so, however, was coming very soon.

The debut of my first workshop was attended by individuals and friends with whom I had already been sharing my gifts. They wanted to hear and learn more about making change happen. I am a firm believer in vision boards and have used them for years in many different capacities. I felt led to create a model that included the steps of: Envision, Release, Manifest, and Gratitude (which would later be changed to Receive). This activity has been one that develops vision and strengthens mission as well as purpose. As Michael Beckwith shared, "Knowing your purpose and living your purpose are two very distinct things." We still use this workshop today, in a new format with additional experiences included. I look at the path from where I have come, and I cannot believe the beautiful way in which I have been honored by its unfolding. It all begins with simply adopting a new way of viewing the life you have and the life you want to live. As you begin to envision your life, your day, your work, your outreach, and your family, you are taking the first step in setting intention. It is examining where you are now and where you want to find yourself in the future, being willing to open up and allow it all to unfold.

> *"Ask and you shall receive,*
> *knock and the door shall be open."*
> —Matthew 7:7

When we ignite intention, we create a positive flow of energy, which in turn pulls toward us things charged with positive energy. When using affirmations, for example, we place our intended knowledge, beliefs, and actions into positive terms to attract what we desire to see manifested the most. Life is designed to be ignited and slowly sparked when we are ready, willing, and able to call it forth. Saying you want something to occur in your life and actually taking action to make it happen are two very different things. God wants what is good for us, not what is harmful or negative. His intention is always our best intention. As we begin to ignite intentions to "step up" into life, we need to focus on doing so with ease, grace, synchronicity, and serendipity. Let life be the spark toward its alignment to you. Let it not be forced by you. Can you hear the difference in the words of those two sentences?

> *"Some of the best things I've attracted have happened*
> *unexpectedly because I clearly knew the WHAT,*
> *but I didn't push the HOW."*
> —Christine Kane

As you wake up in the morning, even before stepping out of bed, focus on the day before you. Envision it in its newness and greatest glory of co-creation. You will activate this in your life with intentional steps. For now, take a moment to breathe in your I AM's and breathe out your I AM NOT's, releasing your chains and anchors as you are claiming your purpose. Whether you pray or meditate, acknowledge and celebrate God's hand in your life. Feel the warmth of love in each breath for the day is ready to unfold.

Intention isn't about the motive of power in our walk
but the purpose behind the steps.
Flats can walk forward just as well as heels
as you set intention in each day.

Past focus has wired us to see life and work as something to be achieved, not received. The masculine version of intention is filled with the old ways of setting goals and outcomes, determining the push of "power" and influence to ensure the highest level of abundance and worth. The feminine energy of *allowing* brings forth the ease and acceptance of what is unfolding, with the attraction of positive intention, lifting us to higher purpose. Learning to balance the two is key, with maximum energy given to the feminine focus.

The Steps of Igniting Powerful Intentions

Step one is **ENVISIONING**. This is different than seeing or viewing. Envisioning is an action involving the mind, body, and spirit. It is both BE and DO simultaneously. It requires the feeling of the present and the hopefulness of the future. Giving intentional thought to each day will consist of actively following these "I" statements and steps:

I am....
I will....
I wonder....
I dedicate....

You may choose to state it out loud and/or write it down in a planner or journal. Choose an **I AM** statement you have already written that resonates with you for today or one you are currently developing. Either one will work! Your **I WILL** defines your focus, your active part, the "doing" part of your day that involves the allowing and blossoming of actions to take place. The **I WONDER** is full of opportunities, new doors, and the hope that's ignited by the excitement of the adventure. **I DEDICATE** is a way to offer your day as one lived in honor or memory of someone close to you. This brings a feeling of legacy into our work.

How can you "step up" into life when you don't know what to expect? To answer that, live life intentionally! It involves having faith in your co-creation of life each day. It is powerful, yet gentle, and stabilizes us to move forward in life one step at a time.

> Intention aids in eliminating the fear of the unknown.

Our inner desire of purpose leads us to motivation, yet it's important to note that our desire must be unattached to the outcome or the "how" of something occurring. If we are attached to what will result or a specific way it must play out for us to experience happiness, this becomes a craving in life, not a desire. Unfortunately, we may experience suffering as a byproduct. We want to focus on the feelings we are desiring, so the outcomes will be better received.

Step two is **RELEASE**. The fear of resistance is real. Staying unattached to how our intentions manifest, however, is key to our desires remaining the focus. The push and pull in life, the things that keep us from pursuing our dreams, like fear of not being enough, fear of judgement or success, and all the other "what if's" we tend to create, only block us from truly receiving what is intended for us. Stress can either be the "story" of our lives or it can be a catalyst of joy and hope. The choice is up to us.

My mantra has been to *Release to Receive*. Let's walk through an exercise together. Close your eyes and picture a clenched hand or fist holding on dearly to the things you believe are important in life, gripping them with a tightness so as not to drop or lose the contents resting firmly on your palm. Did you squeeze your fist securely? What things did you imagine yourself holding onto? Feel the weakened energy in your hand given to fear, instead of gently holding something with reverence. At that moment of firmly gripping, if I had offered you an amazing gift, one you have always wanted, would you have been able to accept it? Would you have been open to receive it in the moment? Likely not. Therefore, you must be willing to release things that may not be serving you any longer and may not even be positive anymore, to receive the new, fabulous, and desired gifts waiting just ahead.

We all hold on to individuals or groups, memories, belongings, jobs, unhealthy habits, and many other things that once held value in our lives. This grip of fear or sense of lack prevents us from releasing what no longer benefits us to receive the newness of blessings and the abundance that awaits. What are you willing to *Release to Receive*?

Step three is **MANIFEST**. Manifesting is bringing forth who you really are and what purpose you are creating along this journey. It is the faith in allowing your life to unfold in its truest form and at its highest potential, recognizing and using your own gifts as necessary pieces in expanding yourself. You are amazingly unique, and you direct the steps of our incredible path of creativity. It is important each day to open the door to creative connections through your mind, body, and spirit. Many of us think of creativity as developing something new, like a song, poem, painting, or novel. However, creativity is much more than that. Without it, we wouldn't be able to work or solve problems in our daily lives. All of us have the capacity to be creative. Our brains are pre-wired for it from birth. Just watch a young child as they actively engage in all things sensory. Colors, smells, sounds, images, tastes, and feelings all come alive. Knowing it is that im-

> We never lose our sense of wonder and curiosity.

portant, what do you do to engage in creativity? Are you actively involved in creativity or is it an area that needs to be enhanced in your life?

As you will find, we have placed some fabulous coloring pages and poetry within the chapters of this book. They are the artistic creations of a friend and colleague, Marvia Davidson. (You may find her information in the back pages.) The quotes are ones she found within this book, and the hand lettering and designs are her own inspired originals. Hope you enjoy her work as much as I do! As you can probably guess, I've already colored my pages.

We know there is a powerful link between creativity and positive emotions, which ultimately leads to happiness. Have you ever found it less likely to feel negative emotions, such as, fear, anger, sadness, and anxiety, when being in your creative mode? You can see that truth amplified when activating your creativity while feeling joyful, loving, and curious. It causes you to experience more interest and fascination with the world around you. When you allow yourself to explore, observe, and discover, you will feel open and alive. That is what will draw you in to learn new skills, perspectives, and ideas, evoking new opportunities and solving challenges that may be in the way. It will even boost your resilience and satisfaction with life, both of which are important parts of the equation for overall happiness.

How do we engage in being more creative to manifest our dreams and ideas in life? I find the mind, body, spirit connection and alignment to be our most powerful asset. I have used yoga for myself and for children and teens for years. As a principal, I designed the school day to begin with yoga. Even the parents would stay around to participate with us. The teachers felt it helped center our children better through increased focus, interest, creativity, and happier moods. Breath is a major foundation in yoga, and we used breathing techniques with our children every day. Deep breathing is relaxing and is a supportive, as researched in numerous medical studies, in positively affecting your heart, brain, digestion, immune system, and possibly even cell development. We can help create a positive system with the ability to release the hold of stress and its effect on us.

> *"As long as you are breathing,
> there is more right with you than wrong."*
> —Jon Kabat Zinn

When I work, coach, or even facilitate a workshop or event, I always plan the environment in advance to be inviting for all in attendance. We enter an environment through our senses first, so paying close attention to the five senses is key. I think about what the environment will look like, sound like, feel like, smell like, and even taste like. Take a moment to reflect on possible aspects you could enhance in your work or life environment to better support you.

The final component of manifesting is found in the simplicity of life. I call it "balance and bliss." It appears in the stolen moments between *being* and *doing*. When you establish what balance in life works for you, joy becomes evident and quite attainable in that balance. Perhaps working from nine a.m. to five p.m., taking an hour for lunch and a couple of fifteen-minute breaks to breathe or stretch your legs balances your energy. If so, great! I would just encourage you to find something blissful or joyful to engage in over your lunch and during those shorter breaks. Sometimes eating your lunch outside with a friend or walking to and from the smoothie shop for a healthy stretch, while verbalizing affirmations of your I AM's, will work just beautifully.

Balance and bliss is ever-present in my days with my grandchildren, my husband, our family, and dear friends. Quality time spent just being present in wonder and curiosity is my "happy place." That may involve traveling, writing, being outdoors, and much more. One day a week with our grandson we are very "in-the-moment" of his routines of play, embracing his unique and changing needs and admiring his glimpses of wonder. As I write this, I can share this week's memorable moment with you. My little guy, Clark, my husband, and I were playing outside when Clark suddenly remembered the sand table in our backyard and its contents. He flung off the lid and dove into the table retrieving all of the treasured items he had not played with for a while. He immediately launched into making motor engine sounds of the construction trucks, paired with little dinosaurs who were needing a ride to cross the vast side of the bridge constructed of rocks. I was drawn in as usual with my own vehicle and dinosaur, as we conversed about the long journey. My husband was laughing and said, "Honey, I've been calling you for the last few minutes, and you didn't even hear me." I responded with a look of "Really?" and we both chuckled together. I was in full blown *balance and bliss,* and so was Clark, dinosaurs, motor sounds and all.

Where's your *balance and bliss*? It is time for you to investigate its whereabouts and visit there often, so you know what it feels like when you most likely need it. Make a list of your favorite balance experiences and what stolen moments of bliss that make your heart feel full. I know I need to visit those places often...every week and a lot of moments in between. You will read even more about balance and bliss in the section entitled Simplicity Signals later in this chapter. It is one of the most important pieces to walking with purpose in your life.

Step four, and the most important, is **RECEIVE**. Gratitude is the step in which we honor our blessings and those of others. Yet, it is the step that sometimes is the most forgotten in our lives.

My mom was a voracious reader, and I shared that passion with her. We were always sharing books and talking about the ones we were reading. She was way before her time, as she would read the writings of authors she had just seen an article about and then order the book to read later before the day had ended. Even as a Christian deeply rooted in her faith, she would read things such as Eckhart Tolle, Marianne Williamson, and Deepak Chopra, who weren't always aligned with her beliefs. It did help her in broadening her views and appreciating new ideas and insights. I was raised with these out-of-the-box ways of thinking and have always pushed the barriers to what everyone else sees and believes. I guess I follow her beliefs even more today through my own Christian spiritual faith.

I remember very vividly in 1995, Mom watched a show where Sarah Ban Breathnach's new book, *Simple Abundance,* was being featured. This author was such a believer in being thoughtful, grateful, and appreciative of life and others, and her book resonated with my mother's spirit. Together, we decided to begin the practice of individually journaling our gratitude in Sarah's journal. It was a profound moment when, years later, after Mom passed, I found and read her journal. The moments of gratitude for the simplest of things was revealed. I was so happy we had taken that journey years ago to start a practice of gratefulness every day, no matter what the circumstances. When my father passed away, my mom's entries were ones of "receiving" the little joys of moments past and present. A sunset, a conversation with a friend, a call from me at the end of the day just to chat, the birds singing so beautifully in the backyard trees...Mom had recorded them all.

If you have not taken a gratitude journey, Sarah Ban Breathnach's books, *Simple Abundance: A Daybook of Comfort and Joy, Something More: Excavating Your Authentic Self,* and *The Simple Abundance Journal of Gratitude,* are very highly recommended. I quote, "Sarah's work celebrates quiet joys, simple pleasures, and well-spent moments. By reminding us to search for the small and the sweet in our daily round with appreciation and awe, we find the beauty in the everyday. *Simple Abundance* is also responsible for introducing two concepts—the 'gratitude journal' and the term 'authentic self' into the American conversation." Mom and I would agree.

Receiving is the final component to Igniting Intention. How can we walk with purpose if we are not grateful for each step along the path, whether they were ones of stumbling or celebrating? When we receive all the marvelous things we have been given, even before they happen, miracles will occur. Gratitude each day and each step on your path is crucial to your new purpose.

Sometimes when searching for answers we have to acknowledge what we appreciate in our lives to move from feeling the negative energies of lack to witnessing the positive feelings in one sigh of fullness. What is the very best part of today? How will tomorrow bring even more abundance and moments to take your breath away?

Outside the window,
Out past the lawn,
Sweet night was snuggling
Soft as a yawn.
All small ones home now
To burrow, to hedge, to nest.
All babes in bed now
For cuddles, stories and rest.
As we climb into bed
Get ready to play
Our favorite game called
"The best part of the day!"
—Sarah Ban Breathnach , *The Best Part of the Day*

You know I love movies and children's stories. What a wonderful routine for every parent or grandparent to end the day with their children! What's the best part of your day?

Give thanks for the blessing of each moment, each spark of something new, each breath spent in new excitement, and each ping of a little pain. They are all just a piece of the new journey you are walking.

What am I grateful for? I am grateful for YOU, reading and walking this story with me.

I am grateful for the time you have chosen to be with me and reflect on your own life. I am grateful for the opportunity to be just a little part of your journey. I am grateful for you as you participate in this experience of life of igniting intention through envisioning, releasing, manifesting, and receiving. Bring for your gratitude in each day as your visions unfold. It is the PROCESS of life, NOT the PRODUCT. The best is yet to come. Shine your "flashlight" brightly and glow baby, glow!

Here is my example of how I put these steps into action in my life. My igniting of intention had occurred; I was releasing my fears; I was manifesting the new dreams into action; and I was so grateful for what God had already revealed in my life. Doing the work on myself to have a balance of learning how to BE and who I was/am with my DO of putting the new insights into action. I was ready to STEP UP.

It was in these first baby steps I made the decision to attend a networking event of a women's organization I had been a part of online for a couple of years. The chapter president was having a sharing evening of our companies, services, and products to let others know what we do. I felt the gentle nudging to attend and take a chance on sharing my new endeavor with these women I didn't know. Recently, I took a step UP and launched a very simple new company called, something super original for the time being, LLD Legacy. LLD are my initials and Legacy was what I wanted to leave to my current family and to honor my family that had all passed. Their memory was important to me. My degrees paired with my certifications and passions in coaching, consulting, and training were going to come to new use.

That night I met some fabulous women, mostly entrepreneurs and some with careers. It made me feel like I belonged somewhere right now. My first introduction was to Eileen, a woman who was previously an RN and partnered in a consulting firm focused on using brain-based and medically sound strategies to support C-level and mid-management individuals to perform at their optimum level by reducing the effects of stress and poor physiological patterns. It was like finding a kindred spirit in my first passion of neuroscience. We bonded that night over our work and our insights on how spiritual concepts all intersect how we live and work. Just what I had always wanted to do…bring my beliefs and background together. My journey took yet another step UP into my new purpose. Just one little step led to a foothold to put my next step into motion. Little did I know this relationship and these women would turn into a fabulous partnership later, one which would bring my purpose and passions to an even broader opportunity, one of alignment, learning, connections, and even collaboration. This first step UP was a very important one.

> *To walk the intentional journey, take one step at a time. Breathe it in, feel the path under your feet, and appreciate it no matter what it may feel like.*

ILLUMINATION INSIGHT: *Embracing Change*

> *Change is situational. Transition is psychological. Transformation is reflective and soul-filled.*

Am I feeding into my fear through a shattered lens of life? Or am I looking through a clear and shining one? That all depends on how we reframe our lives during moments of transition and transformation. Even when you are moving toward your dreams and passions, life has a way of teaching you to appreciate both the times of health and the times of illness. As the scripture found in Ecclesiastes 3 states, "There is a time for everything, and a season for every activity under the heavens." The recurrence of my illness was one my doctors could not yet explain. They decided to put me back on very drastic medication, and it was a trial-and-error type of method. I wasn't yet able to decipher how to work with this shift in my life.

I hear on a regular basis, "Life is so hard. Why can't it be easier? No one has challenges like I do." Yes, we all feel like we live on "leper island" during certain seasons of our lives. It is in these very seasons, however, that we learn the much-needed strength of resiliency. Can we truly rewire our thinking? The answer is a resounding YES! When we are plagued by the constant feelings and thoughts of negativity, compiled by a disbelief that things will change in our lives any time soon, we may benefit from picking up the facts, along with the feelings we are experiencing, and placing them inside a new frame. This requires a deliberate shift in focus from the list of negative examples of how it won't ever happen for you to a positive, life-centered focus on how you can create the outcome you desire. What is in your power to change?

Our own perceptions are powerful! What we "view" and bring into focus becomes our reality. As a matter of fact, we can even convince ourselves that a carrot is a tiger. An even more vivid example is in *Peter Pan* when he is with the Lost Boys having a feast. Just by thinking about and imagining the most outrageously decadent food and desserts, a buffet suddenly materializes and Peter sees it despite his aging eyes.

My husband and I love movies, and Disney is definitely one of our happy places! It is where dreams really do come true, don't you think? I don't mean commercial dreams, but dreams where imagination, determination, and vision lie. Do you believe our imaginations and creative thoughts can actually bring forth a whole new reality? If not, maybe it's time for you to start believing. Imagination is required in setting the powerful intentions in life. Have you ever heard of Imagineers? They are the artists, directors, and managers for Disney World and Disneyland. These extraordinary individuals exercise their "muscles" in this way every day by bringing the unbelievable to life, literally. Imagineers not only dream, but also create as they put into action the things they imagine. If you don't believe yet, try asking a three-year-old if pretending works. You have not lost this ability just because you've grown up and become an adult. You simply might have stopped utilizing that part of your brain. The brain is a muscle that requires exercising to get stronger and build endurance. So, the more often you practice using your imagination, the easier it will become. Imagining IS the window to creatively designing our future and its outcomes. Walt Disney felt that language could create or kill an idea or a vision. I believe he was correct! So, take care to align your speech, as well, with the dreams and visions you are imagining for your life

Embracing Change through Language

> *"As we say, small shifts create seismic differences."*
> —Dr. Kathryn Cramer

Have you ever told a young child NOT to do something, and then watched as they immediately proceeded to act out the very thing you warned them not to do? We are wired to hear what to DO, rather than what NOT to do. The brain has to learn to hear the action and then turn it around to say, "No, don't do it." Wouldn't it just be easier to tell someone what you *want* them to do, including yourself? I have shared in many instances the power of positive based language in our lives. We carry these powerful words with us throughout life, but we also carry the negative ones, which bear a heavier weight. Change must occur in our lives through language that is paired with our actions. Change is always a challenge, and sometimes we believe it is something someone else should do, instead of us. How can we best respond when change is required? We must shift the way we think and feel about it. We can free ourselves from past and present anger, fear, pain, and loss, and see tomorrow as an opportunity to take one step toward change.

Practicing with new language and shifting focus toward "what's working" in life more than "what isn't working" assists us in overcoming life's challenges and hurdles. In 2015, I was blessed to partner with two international best-selling authors, Dr. Kathryn Cramer and Hank Wasiak. Their mentoring was powerful for not only me to experience but the clients we were able to reach in numerous industries in order to create change. The psychology behind our work, researched and started by Dr. Cramer, was called Asset-Based Thinking™, or better known as ABT. Creating mindsets of seeing ourselves, others, and situations differently which allows us to operate in our personal inner power, influence, impact, as we see the future through growth "lenses." Seeing ABT in action is seeing seismic differences and embracing change, especially through our language.

Have you ever started learning a new skill or implementing a healthy habit, such as walking or running? There are many new apps to help those wanting to set a goal of participating in a local charity walk or run yet haven't been in training to know how to prepare for this goal to be successful. One of these apps with a fabulous success rate is known for taking its users from being couch potatoes to marathon runners. How does that happen exactly? To answer that question, it's accomplished by taking one step at a time toward the new goal and raising the intention to gradually increase the steps with each new day. Stepping up requires conditioning and increased strength to be able to build stamina and endurance for the length and intensity necessary to accomplish new goals. It challenges you to be BRAVE in your steps. Brave work leads to an outcome of courage, even though you may feel afraid or uncertain. When you gain the ability to step out in faith and purpose, it just feels different. Courage is that strength that is found in the quiet and stillness of life, the moments where you dig deep and resolve to say, "I can do this!"

I receive frequent questions from others about, "What's my purpose in life?" or "How do I find out about...?" I usually respond with, "One step at a time." Discover who you are, what you want, and what your biggest hurdles are to overcome. Waiting for purpose to just appear one day is futile. You must continue to take those baby steps and find where to place each foot. Feel life change for you and others in the process, and your purpose will be revealed in time. It isn't a cerebral activity where massive thinking is required. It is a mind, body, and spirit alignment, and lies deep within your core. Trust it!

Brenda was a new client of mine, a creative young hair stylist with a desire to travel and do hair for up-and-coming high-end clients. She came to me with the goals of owning her own salon or traveling to do hair nationally. She was trying to make a decision about what was to come next and needed help deciding between the two visions. I listened intently to what she said, which would reveal not only her "head"-felt intentions, but also her "heart"-felt ones. That's where our visionary opportunities begin. I gave her the "I AM" list of at least ten statements as homework and couldn't wait until the next week when we would meet to hear her answers. Her list began:

"I am an entrepreneur."
"I am creatively talented."
"I am shy and sometimes have social anxiety."
"I am strong and have been living on my own since I was fifteen."

"I am an over thinker."
"I am a supportive sister."

When she came to the next sentence, her voice struggled some to utter the words, "I am beautiful." Why did she struggle? I let her finish, and I listened. She shared how hard it was for her to say those words. She knew in her head that she was beautiful, yet she had difficulty accepting those words for herself.

As you read above, some of her statements also revealed challenges in her life. I asked her, "Why did you choose to be a stylist?" Her answer was lovely and sincere. She replied that making other women feel beautiful by doing their hair gave her value and passion in life. Women needed to be cared for and pampered, and she helped meet that need, as they heard her words of beauty for them. She gave me example after example of how she would stroke their hair, washing, drying, coloring, styling, and cutting, while speaking words of affirmation she wishes others had given her. What a mission!

I then asked her to talk me through a list of "I AM NOT's." As she read each statement the fury poured out and her voice strengthened. Her articulation and tone became louder and more precise.

"I AM NOT ugly."
"I AM NOT fat."
"I AM NOT stupid or a woman who won't amount to anything."
"I AM NOT worthless, where no one will want me."
"I AM NOT damaged or someone who can't be fixed."

Who had uttered those words to her? Who, in their own feelings of lack, jealousy, envy, or negativity, instilled those mental and emotional barriers into a young girl, teen, or woman? I shared with her that these are examples of lies she had heard others speak about her and tried desperately not to believe. These had become anchors in her soul. At times we have all heard similar lies from people we have trusted, people who loved us and were a part of our journey for a long time. They created a deep and hurtful impact and a belief system in us that was inaccurate. They were spoken over us when we were just learning about self-identity, worth, and self-love. We made choices in our relationships based on how those words made us feel about ourselves. Have you ever chosen someone to be in a relationship with someone, whether it was a friend or a love interest, who wasn't good for you or negatively affected you in some way? There could be a deeper cause for this.

We remember what others say about us negatively at a sensory and cellular level. It is embedded deep in our psyche and works, sometimes, as a protective shield, making it difficult for positive statements to break through. As Rick Hansen states in his book *The Buddha's Brain*, "Negative thoughts, feelings, and actions are like Velcro to our brains, and positive ones are like Teflon." The negative ones we tend to more easily own and believe, whereas the positive ones we often doubt. When I was studying this phenomenon for my work in Asset-Based Thinking and my own dissertation, I held on to the work by Dr. Barbara Friedman entitled, *Bad is Stronger than Good*. What a statement to make! We have always been led to believe that good always wins, that good is stronger and will outweigh any bad situation. Yet, for that to ring true, we first must overcome and shift the hold on the negative mindset we previously believed. When we fully realize we need to feed the positive thoughts, feelings, and actions more than we do the negative ones, we begin to see the change we each desire. Dr. John Gottman, in his research of negative and positive thinking, communication, and behavior, shares a fundamental truth. To shift a negative thought to a positive one, we must place five times more emphasis on the positive, thus, creating what is known as the 5:1 ratio. For example, the next time you have a challenge or a negative thought, try giving five ways it will work, five positive solutions, or five more times to try it. You will soon begin to feel and see the shift occur.

With the example of Brenda, these I AM NOT statements were "Velcroed" to her very soul. Shifting her mindset to not just KNOW the positives aspects about herself, but also to believe and OWN the statements would be some of our next steps. Imagine how the tears of release flowed as she learned to walk out of the comfort zone and release the fear of living life being judged, shamed, and tossed aside. She embraced herself with words and feelings of acceptance and honor. These words of affirmation were powerful.

> Many times, our greatest growth in life, as well as our most immense pleasure, comes from change.

---

*"Self-love, self-respect, self-worth.
There's a reason they all start with 'self.'
You can't find them in anyone else."*
—Unknown

Change isn't always negative or painful. It can often be very pleasant and unexpected. I learned an important lesson about change from my rescue kitty, Olivia. Change is a fluid and unavoidable part of life that needs to be accepted and embraced.

In one instance, change came for us in the form of a new life and an unexpected furry addition to our family, which was not in our plan. My husband and I were driving one day when we noticed a small animal trying to cross a very busy intersection. As we watched, we noticed the car in front of us hit the small animal and toss its lifeless body to the gutter. My husband and I realized it was a Calico kitten and pulled our car over to a parking lot. We ran with towels in hand to confirm what we had seen and try to help. The tiny kitten took off in great fear, dragging the back of her body. We were able to capture her and swaddle her in the towel. I brought her close to my chest with her little face looking up at me. Such fear, crisis, and trauma turned within moments into safety and protection. It was in those moments that the love affair began.

We immediately drove the kitten to our vet, where he confirmed the internal organs were undamaged, yet her back leg was broken in three places. If she was going to make it, we would have to adopt her and provide a high level of care. I relied on friends to help me quickly find a travel crate to bring her home, and I then made a happy dash to the local pet store to purchase it, along with toys, kitten food, and kitten milk. The decision was made, so with a large cast and a frightened five-week-old "fur baby" in tow, I started home. With my husband working, I learned a new schedule of routine four-hour feedings with a syringe, how to give medication to a kitten, and how to swaddle and rock her to sleep. My husband and I have enjoyed hours of laughing together and watching her explore new environments and experiences with great curiosity. Our lives have been forever changed because an unexpected tragedy turned into a blessing.

Princess Olivia, as we lovingly call her, ended up having overwhelming neurological and physical challenges as she got older. We knew she would never be able to go outside, but she would always have a home full of love and fun with us. Olivia, in her time of crisis and great need, changed our lives forever. So, when you are asking for change to occur or need something new in your life to assist you in your acceptance of joy, you may just receive a small gift that will shift the way you look at everything. Be watching and EMBRACE IT!

Change is inevitable. It is whether or not we choose to embrace it, receive it, and make it part of the new journey, that determines its benefit or detriment. On the path involving my health challenges, change is a regular occurrence, being that I experience strange "attacks" on my body, called "flares," due to the autoimmune cycle. During one such lengthy flare, my back and the nerves leading into my leg were affected. We were expecting our next grandchild, and the excitement surrounding this event was grand! It was the first boy to be brought into our family! As we all prepared for his birth, my body decided to follow with extreme pain and decreased ability to walk even the shortest distances. After numerous doctor visits, physical therapy sessions, and other alternative options, as well, the change was minimal and came with tremendous challenge. The verdict was quite drastic, and the remedy didn't even ensure a positive result of walking again without pain or the possibility of collapsing.

During a sobering visit with my back surgeon, whom had already performed a major back surgery and numerous injections, I shared through tears with him my hope and prayer...I just wanted to be able to walk my grandson's stroller around the block on a sunny day and to be able to put him in the crib upstairs in our home. He shed tears of understanding with me. That day, I walked out of my surgeon's supportive office back into physical therapy and began working with water therapy, one of my favorite forms of exercise and healing. I made it my intention every morning for two months to walk my grandson's stroller around the block. I later added the intention to walk the hospital hallways when he was born. Well, did I walk without pain? No. Still, I chose to shift my own mindset toward believing that I could do what I needed to, moving forward and stepping up into my intentions of walking, playing, and moving again. Rev. Michael Bernard Beckwith shares it so well, "We can choose to grow in life through pain or we can grow through insight. We need both in life to move forward. There is a choice in each situation we encounter." Which will you choose?

ILLUMINATION INSIGHT: Creating Confidence and Courage

Walt Disney World and Disneyland were created through the "Yes, if..." approach to deal making. Creative people thrive on "Yes, if..." statements in their work. Disney was quoted saying, "Somehow I can't believe that there are many heights that can't be scaled by a (wo)man who knows the secret of making dreams come true. The special secret can be summarized in four C's. They are Curiosity, Confidence, Courage, and Constancy, and the greatest of these is Confidence. When you believe a thing, believe in it all the way. Have confidence in your ability to do it right and work hard to do the best possible job." That is the difference. It is in the choice of believing and using positive language to support you in the process that goals are attained and dreams become realities.

Michael Hyatt, author of *Your Virtual Mentor*, believes everyone, and especially leaders, have days filled with positive and negative experiences. "Challenges are constant, but confidence is not. It comes and goes." He shares that people often experience the greatest doubt and anxiety at the start of something big, whether it is good or bad. Most would agree. Once you are moving forward, stepping OUT and stepping UP into purpose, you gain momentum and bring your prior successes with you. Keep in mind, you also bring your failures, too. However, realizing that failure is merely a lesson learned makes the difference. You can carry with you the lesson *or* the doubt and pain, which will only create an abrupt halt in your progress. The choice is yours.

Courage is stepping out of the comfort zone and taking one step UP...whether we are successful, or we fail miserably, we still foster courage. We get up and we do it again, learning lessons along the way. It is accepting and allowing courage to develop that causes us to grow, not the pushing and pulling, which creates resistance. That will only lead to fear. Confidence and courage are both required if we are desiring to further develop and grow in our lives, yet not without understanding the concepts of "knowing and owning." *Knowing* is the level awareness in our lives. *Owning* is when you feel it and believe it to be truth in your life. Let me illustrate a few examples of how these two components work to build confidence and courage.

At one time in my work, I had the honor of bringing a specialized curriculum to a large group of teens in an alternative program. They were completing a school-based, credit-recovery program in hopes of finishing their high school diploma, and this new curriculum involved shifting mindset and growing individual strengths. Their counselors, therapists, and teachers were with us as we engaged in high-level experiences in leadership. It is important to mention that these young people, ages sixteen to eighteen, were desperately trying to walk away from desperate life circumstances. Many were coming out of addiction, had been dealing drugs or involved in gangs, or found themselves overcoming a legacy of poverty, illiteracy, abuse, or domestic violence. Some of these teenagers were living on the streets or in their cars, and others had children of their own, supporting themselves and their children with outside jobs. The school was located on the border of Mexico, and the influence of family challenges on the other side of the border, was overwhelming for many of them. The personnel that supported them were some of the most caring and dedicated I have ever met. Their heartfelt mission was to give these young people a new start at a brand-new life. Leadership initiatives were key for them.

We were facilitating an activity in which the youth were asked to create a star-shaped art design with each point of the star representing an area of their personal positive-based characteristics, such as, mind, body, spirit, and others. Most of the students loved the openness and creative opportunity to share their own insights about themselves. One young girl was the exception and actually laid her head down on her table and refused to participate. When I prompted her with each point of the star to find a confident place for her to begin, she would shrug her shoulders. When her friends would support her with words to help her fill in the areas, she doubted them and would even say, "really" in disbelief. After a conversation we had, she said she heard what we said about her but did not see those qualities in herself. What a powerful statement for us all!

The lessons these insightful youth provided were intense. I hope you will indulge me in one more story of these young people with profound statements that impacted my journey forward. A young male student named Juan was asked what being focused on your strengths more than your weaknesses, your I AM's more than your I AM NOT's, meant to him. We also wanted to have him share how the experiences affected him during our time together. So, he replied with deep emotion and intensity, "You are the first person in my life that has shown me what I CAN do, what I AM good at, and told me that I CAN make a difference." I asked him what he usually heard, and he stated, "that I'm not going to amount to anything, that I can't do anything, and I will never be successful in school or in life." Powerful words! I still remember them today with such sensory image and detail.

> Knowing what others see or believe is very different than "owning" it and believing it within yourself.

His teachers were in the audience watching the discussion with tears streaming. I was shocked. After the session was completed with the student group, I met with the teachers to debrief. The teachers shared that the comment had changed the way they saw the efforts from a student perspective. They continued to share how all of the comments made them feel and how ashamed they felt. The realization as a team was how they intended for the statements they made to students to be supportive. For instance, they may have stated the student might not be successful if he or she doesn't start participating in school or the student won't amount to anything, unless they have a high school diploma. Their shift in perspective came when they realized they never meant for their students to focus on the first statement they would share with them, but the last statement. This is a profound example of how the student only heard the negative statement. This particular student "owned" the words of "lack" because it matched his mindset of himself and past experiences in school. This deep insight was the first step in true personal change!

What has your past told you? What barriers to intention have been placed on you so stepping UP feels like a struggle? Personal change happens for all of us, no matter what our past, where we are in the present; we each have just as much opportunity in the future. It is our choice how to embrace it, believe it, and own it for ourselves.

SIMPLICITY SIGNALS

As we illumine our way to "step up," we will find having a few strategies to enlist will be helpful in the process. They are tried and true "signals" to use as needed, however often that may be for you. I hope they are useful on your journey, I know they were and still are on mine.

Pressing Pause Moment

When you are engaged fully in walking your path, you will experience moments of necessary pausing. You may need to just breathe and meditate before making choices or examining options. It may be an opportunity to readjust and gather new insights or to release some fear or other negative emotions, individuals, and even situations. Pause for moments, hours, or even a day before returning to action. Take the press pause moment and use as needed, however often. It will assist you in regaining insight, energy, and balance between movement. Staying on the path is important so you do not revert all the way back to the comfort zone, unless it is necessary.

Rewind, Reset, and Reframe

How do we **rewind**? If you look down at a TV remote in your hand or a music app on your phone, you will see a rewind arrow going backwards. You can review, reset, and release what has passed in order to move forward. You may choose to bring a positive strategy with you or a dream or memory you want to remember in this moment. A rewind can give you deep insight on past lessons allow you to gather strength from them to move along. It is how you view this "rewind" experience that determines whether it works for you or works against you. If it works "against" you it means you brought forward a negative aspect of the past, a hurt, fear, or painful piece, and it will affect whether you move in a new direction. This is reset and reframe come into action. Be careful on your choices. It is only a rewind for a backward glance, not a "vacation" in the past.

What is a **reset**? When you cannot gain a good connection with an electronic device, what do you do? You reset. Go back to original setup that you know well. It's a neutral and stationary place in life. Sometimes when we face challenges or new territory in life, we need to stay neutral to gather more information and reset our life to a new normal before moving forward again. It is important to not view something or someone as negative or positive and even staying in a place of no decision until we can gather more information. We tend, as humans, to rush into judgement and fear when we don't understand. The adrenaline rush and even "addiction" is powerful for us to choose negative and either fight, run away, or hide out. Reset allows us the breath to remain neutral until we understand more before moving forward. We then want to move into the stage or strategy of reframing.

A **reframe** is how we move from negative or neutral to positive. After we gather more insight, we can adjust our view of the individual, situation, or place as we see how points align or misalign to us. We use positive language to shift our perspective and make a decision from a place of calmness and with full connection to mind, body, and spirit. For instance, seeing someone you work with as egotistical, narcissistic, demanding, and judgmental may create a deep connection to someone you encountered previously and how they hurt you or created a negative situation for you. You may want to judge them, talk about them, ignore them, or even use verbal displays of sarcasm and battle words against them. Instead, choose to reframe the person and the situations in a different light, one of neutral shifting to positive. See them as strong, empowered, knowing who they are, willing to speak their own truth, and yet possibly not experiencing how to connect with others more positively. You may choose to model how to speak about others in a positive way. Remember, it is their lesson, their journey. Yours is to reframe their interaction with you and keep going. See the difference. Your mind, body, and spirit will stay in alignment with your true purpose.

Balance and Bliss

As I shared earlier in this chapter, balance and bliss as well as self-care are necessary components to stepping UP and maintaining forward momentum. Planning for and engaging in this *Simplicity Strategy* will determine your success. I have always found children and nature to be so grounding and elevating, which is where balance and bliss lies.

As I write today, I am inspired by my environment and who I am spending my time within this moment. My husband and grandson are playing in the sand and water table with birds chirping and the sound of running water in the pool. Our little boy is just beginning to really enjoy playing with a definitive purpose with his animals, cars, and kitchen. Engaging in real life play, hearing him babble and talk about it, and watching his interaction with my sweet husband is utterly priceless. He loves to be outside and so do we! Our children today become so inundated with TV, video games, and technology devices even at two years old, so the ability to dig in the dirt, sit in the grass and read books, and play with sticks and rocks is even more important to their development as much as our stress reduction. It IS my balance and bliss! This is why for me my Wednesdays are spent with my husband and my grandson. Since my intentions in healing began around my grandson's birth, it has always been one of my greatest motivators.

Can we find balance and bliss everywhere in our life? Sometimes it can be quite challenging, especially in the midst of great change. Let me share a story of one of those memories in my life.

Remember my shoe passion? Yes, I do find bliss in my shoes, too. My closet was filled with all different kinds of flip flops (of course with sparkles), sandals of every heel height, and only high-heel pumps with the toes out, of course! The toe ring was a consistent item in my life and so was a brilliant pedicure.

After being offered a fabulous dream job at a university in Texas, I felt I could make the shift and move. I always said I would never leave Florida, my family, friends, and my beaches. Yet, the idea of working at an institute in Texas to support my work and research seemed the perfect idea. So, I moved to Dallas! When I asked about beaches, water, palm trees, my university professor colleagues said, "Oh yes, we have those." So, I took the plunge, thought I could handle it, and moved. Well, have you been to Dallas? Yes, the weather is very similar to Florida with the exception of the humidity. Guess what I found out? They all lied! The beaches are over five hours away and so are the palm trees! The water is in the forms of lakes and the sandy, dirty areas surrounding those bodies of water are not and will never be called a beach. So, my balance and bliss environment and practice were gone! Did I also tell you I moved to

Dallas in February, the coldest month of the year here? My second week at my job we had to close for four days due to a snow and ice storm. My poor dog had never seen snow and I have never driven on ice and snow. I was so ready to move home to Clearwater! My balance and bliss were only a memory.

So, what did I do? I got out, once it got warmer, and began appreciating the uniquely warm and friendly culture of Texans. They actually say "hi" to you on the streets even though they may not know you. I loved seeing horses in my daily commute and the wide-open ranches, longhorns, and southern style architecture. After a few months, it did get warmer and I learned what over one hundred degrees feels like. How quickly you make friends when you discuss the weather. My B&B began to shift and walks in places like Katie's Woods around Lake Grapevine and concerts in the park with fireworks during the summer every Friday night started to give me a little of the feeling I left behind with my beach as I wore my flip flops and fit right in. What I realized was I had only traded a little of the shoe collection, which turned into boots, boots, and more boots, just a little Texas humor. I was now embracing my change and walking forward again.

Remember to ignite your intentions each day, breathe IN the moments you are manifesting as you step up to greater and greater work. Use your new strategies of simplicity signals when the need arises.

You are powerful beyond measure. You are a **warrior** (movement manifested, action-oriented, and DO-focused) and a **goddess** (wisdom and intention, reflection and realization, and BE-focused) as you reach through the moments of change for balance and bliss, courage, and confidence in your life.

Walk with Lori: Step UP

How are you stepping UP in life?

What are the hurdles and challenges for you and where are they most prevalent?

How do you activate courage and confidence?

What do you do for self-care to find your own balance and bliss?

chapter five
Step Forward: The Opportunity View

> *"Transformation is a journey from the head to the heart, from scarcity to abundance, from ego to truth, and from fear to love."*
> —Darla LeDoux

For a long time, I've had a desk plaque quote which has inspired my own life and work. It is by Albert Einstein, one of my favorite thinkers and doers of all time. "Out of clutter, find **simplicity**. From discord, find **harmony**. In the middle of difficulty lies **opportunity**." This is where we will be stepping forward into opportunity We will move from the simplicities of life into the harmonies of your voice, through difficulties and fears into the greatest opportunities and realities of your life.

When you step UP and move on, you must be ready for what happens next. We-stepped OUT of the comfort zone, stepped UP onto the path presented. Now it is time to step FORWARD into our new journey as we seek out opportunities driven by intention and lessons through the challenges we encounter. Let's Step Forward together.

Why is opportunity so important to stepping forward in life? As we live, our view will either shift in its clarity, or it will change completely. Maintaining a clear image and staying focused are your most powerful assets during this time. What do you see before you? Does it frighten or comfort you? It may do both. One visualization you can use is to capture a snapshot of a peaceful, calm, relaxing, or inviting image and hold on to it in your mind as you overlay it with what you DO want in your life moving forward. Igniting your intentions and seeing them as you imagine yourself in that environment of bliss and full of opportunity when you need it is powerful. That snapshot can be your first and most important view to hold onto in this process. Follow me as I share a story about my brother-in-law and sister-in-law.

I was blessed to find and marry my soulmate, which also meant marrying into the family, too. He is very close to all of his older brothers and his younger sister as well as numerous cousins. One of his brothers, Paul, and his wife, Sherrie, love to travel the way we do, and we often all go together or meet up at some point in our trips. They travel much more than we do at this time and Sherrie is the queen of always sending postcards showing where they go and what they experience, from museums to caves and everything in between. They are definitely adventurers in their spirit. I collect these postcards and after almost thirteen years of marriage and two years of dating, you can imagine the size of the box! I love to go through the places and new views they have seen and have shared them with others when they need inspiration of a "new view" for their life. Can you close your eyes and imagine a gorgeous location you have been or maybe want to go that's on your bucket list? You've seen it in a magazine or actually stood on its soil. This may have been somewhere you love going and visit frequently with friends or family. Maybe it may be a place you remember from a long time ago even as a child. It was an adventure or dream of yours to be there.

* * *

For me, they did both. The only way I knew how to be responsive, yet patient, was to be observant, mindful, and walk through every door imaginable or offered to me. Could I choose to grasp every new chance to embrace knowledge with an appreciation of my past and my present? That is what I challenge you with in this chapter. Examine your life and be ready for every opportunity.

> When you are looking for new opportunities to come forward, they either come flooding in or they hide and ask you to be mindful and watch for them.

Throughout my life I have been a problem solver. I realized thinking my way through things was the wrong approach after trying repeatedly in some circumstances where I felt the challenge would just straighten or work itself out. Using a balance of thinking and feeling gave me more insight to then move forward. The balance of the two actions was the answer. I began using this process when I would work with clients on identifying their balance between what they wanted and where they were then. Just doing and working harder or thinking harder doesn't mean you will find answers. The heart needs to have a voice when you step forward into opportunity. It can create a cycle of challenge and the action leads to improved thinking, better solutions, more viable options and less heart, less emotional attachment, less balance. When we think about the "teeter totter" of life we can imagine the "what if's" more clearly.

When beginning to interact with new experiences in life, watch the balance of brain and heart, thought and gut. You may even become numb in the process. Saying "no" to the heart creates more dis-ease to the self. Giving a voice to the heart is where we will begin stepping forward. Ask yourself, "How do I feel about that?" as much as, "What do I think about that?"

Your Heart Song

The heart needs its voice. Denying your emotional side and passion is to sacrifice yourself which creates a lack of worth in life. This is why many negative relationships or situations where your voice has been stifled or completely eradicated results in negating your sense of worth.

I have been in relationships that stole my voice and had me follow theirs. Did I plan to choose these types of people? Was it a conscious choice one day to connect with and stay with a person who treated me badly and who controlled my every step? Not at all. Whether it was karma, a lesson in worth, or a pattern from early in life, it doesn't have to affect our heart song, just shift its quality if not identified. For me and for many women, it starts very slowly with someone who sees you and little by little they take care of you, pamper you, spend more and more time with you, don't want you to be alone without them, and begin to create ways to follow what you are doing, who you are with, and how you live your life.

One particular relationship was with a man who slowly maneuvered his way into my life and I ended up engaged to. On the outside, everything appeared fabulous. We had a magnificent home on the beach; I drove a Corvette and had accounts set up at high-end women's boutique and stores. He loved taking me to dinners and trips away skiing and scuba diving. We had a gorgeous boat in a slip nearby and we would be out on it frequently. I worked my normal job and loved what I did every day. I had a company on the side speaking and training on the weekends and summers. I wrote my first book and he was very proud of me, until clients wanted me traveling around the state and country to speak or work with them. That was just a little too far away from him.

Then, it started. He ostracized me from my friends and even would call me repeatedly if I was with my mom for the day. If I wasn't home from work right afterwards, he was checking on me and became more and more angry. He began telling me what to eat, what to wear, how to laugh, and even how to sneeze, a biological function that was altered from extreme stress and has remained to this day. Think of what these types of experiences do to not only our minds, but our bodies, and especially our hearts.

We began to argue a lot, or shall we say, he argued a lot. I began hearing my own voice say, "I'm sorry," even when it wasn't my responsibility. His obsession-compulsive behavior became unmanageable when I would step on a small kitchen rug with long loops and my footprint would remain. He would quickly take the rug and shake it, so no imprint would remain.

Others heard my voice when "I'm sorry" became a mantra for everything, and my colleagues and friends started noticing me becoming quieter and less adventurous. What was happening to me? I became apprehensive and even anxious every day when he came home from work, not knowing which personality he would have each day, loving and supportive or angry and judgmental. My voice and my inner passions were changing. I was constantly in fear of him yet didn't want to lose this "wonderful life" we had, or so I thought. My worth had changed.

Why couldn't this strong woman, who speaks out for others and their value, not speak out for herself? I began to ask myself the same question. My answer came in an unexpected God-incident. We were to start pre-marital counseling to prepare for our upcoming wedding—yes, I was marrying him.

As usual, my fiancé couldn't make the first session, which didn't surprise me, so I went anyway. To my overwhelming blessing, a shift was beginning. I formed a much-needed relationship of confidentiality with my minister/psychologist and I knew I could begin to share my fears, pain, and shifts in perspective that had happened in the six-year relationship we had endured.

My fiancé never attended any of my sessions and with each one I grew stronger and found my rhythm of life again. My voice was returning. I knew what I had to do, but I was warned to act with extreme caution and precision. I began moving my things out slowly to my mom's home without my fiancé noticing. Planning to move into a new place wasn't quite an option because he would know where I was and had already told me I was never allowed to leave, or he would hurt me and bring me back. I couldn't stay at my mom's; he would know where I was, and I didn't want her in the middle. The day came, and I let him know I was moving out and he was not to be at the house when I did. I think he doubted me enough that I felt he would ignore the "threat" of me leaving. Friends were all prepared to help me leave quickly with what I had left to move. I was then staying with a dear friend from church who he didn't know.

I can't tell you the move went smoothly, and the details don't matter. You can only imagine it was one of the most difficult things I physically, mentally, and spiritually endured. Yes, there were threats on my life. But what does matter for you to know is I did reclaim my voice, a voice without fear, without judgement, without a lack of worth, A new voice emerged that resonated with strength, freedom, and new choices and opportunities. This lesson was over, and I was ready to move on to new views in life. Ones which had clarity and purpose and where I knew I would be able to support others going through these transitions and transformations in life, and in fact, I did and still do.

What about you? Is anyone or anything suppressing your voice or its true notes? What voice are you sharing in life? What voice is your true sound and carries the melody of your heart? Let's continue to explore this concept.

I have always loved music! I minored in music and played multiple instruments, including voice, for many years. It was how I connected with God and Spirit. It is how I heard my inner gifts and soothed my soul when necessary. Piano and vocals were my "go-to" sounds. Music and the arts have such connection to the soul. The creativity and imagination are unleashed, and you can hear the vibrational energy in their sounds.

The melody of your heart resonates with your true being, your inner core, your purpose, and as some individuals call it, your "heart seed." I call it your heart song. It is what was given to you when you chose to come to this world at this time. You were needed in this era for a specific reason. I hear these melodies, especially when they are ready to be released, realized, and activated. You hear them too. You hear your own harmony with others when you communicate, both verbally and nonverbally. You feel the sweet connection, or you experience the dissonance of the sounds. Some relationships encourage more music together; others are a moment of interaction with a pleasant ending.

There is a voice you use when you are speaking of your passions in life. This could be your purpose walk and the joy of an inner melody that keeps you walking forward with a personal rhythm. Or, it can be a loving interaction with a significant other or even your children, which results in the harmony of these passionate and loving heart songs. Each has their own unique tone and quality.

Hearing your inner heart song, understanding it, and walking in the truth of its melodies, is what builds self-confidence and courage in certain circumstances. Knowing which individuals and situations bring harmony is what will continue to build and encourage your heart song for you and those around you. We have an internal "GPS" system that guides us toward the energies we need to experience as we strive to walk in harmony and learn from the people, places, and things creating dissonance, so we know the difference and appreciate it.

As you walk forward, you may encounter chords from previous times or circumstance that may or may not still resonate with you in your future. The challenge is to keep moving forward while pausing to understand, learn, reflect, renew, learn, and guide others.

There is a consistent rhythm of the moment that connects to us as we hear a new melody. We may harmonize with others' "heart songs," but only if we appreciate theirs, not expect to change it, and they do the same. A friend recently shared a rather difficult situation with me and entrusted me to hear her feelings and not judge her. I told her: "I hold your heart gently in my hands and hear it beat in the rhythm of your hurt." When the hurt calmed in our conversation, I gently gave her heart back to her. What that means is empathy in the moment we shared—no judgement, no drama, no insights or answers, just pure sharing of a heart song.

Why do we stop using our beautifully gifted and blessed uniqueness found in our heart song? Is it because others have told us it's not enough; it's dumb or ugly; it doesn't sound like everyone else's; it's not what others will want to hear; or it's _____ (you fill in the blank). Are you letting your "giants" and "monsters" get in the way? I know I have. We all have. It is time to let them go. Let's release your beautiful notes and cadence. Breathe in your melody and listen for those opportunities for harmonies in your journey. I can't wait to hear!

The Giants and Monsters that Get in the Way

When you were a young child or even as you grew, did you ever have a fear of something in the closet or under the bed lurking? You knew they were there. At bedtime, you would run as fast as you could and jump into bed, pull up the covers over your head, and lie very still so they didn't know you were there. Most children go through a stage of being scared of the things they cannot see in the dark. Even as adults, we crave how movie directors sensationalize the "scare" factor or the feeling of anticipation by the way they design the lighting, camera angles, and of course, the music. You always know something is coming. We call it entertainment.

The difference in life is there are sometimes no prompts or preparation, except excerpts from the past showing why we need to be afraid. These giants are often in the way of our movements forward in life. They focus our attention on remembering a time when we couldn't, shouldn't, didn't, and wouldn't step forward somehow in our lives. They are the gatekeepers perpetually guarding, not guiding, the way to opportunities. These fears are the anchors in our life that are grounded so deeply we pull with all of our energy and can only move them across the ocean floor ever so slightly. Those giants from the past come forward into our present and are lurking to creep "under our beds and in our closets." They bring shame, blame, judgement, negative self-worth, and many other ugly beliefs with them. The fear they bring is palpable and felt deeply in our heart song of life.

Affirmations are key daily support phrases and a wonderful way of beginning to embrace visions of opportunities and lessen the focus on fears of the "things that go bump in the night." The energy we expend thinking about this could be better expressed somewhere else.

My first affirmation phrase to assist you begins with a story of my dear mentor and friend, Claire. Claire was a brilliant and unique mentor of mine for many years. We became dear friends over the years and I treasure the conversations and insights she shared with me. She had a way of recognizing and bringing out the gifts in others and I was blessed to receive her guidance as I learned more and more about mine. One of the powerful affirmations and strategies she instilled was "accept and dismiss." She would use the phrase repeatedly throughout my life's ups and downs. Claire would calmly and intently listen to what was happening and remind me to accept the thoughts and feelings occurring around me while dismissing the ones that didn't serve the greater good or that in others. Hear, yet don't accept as your own. Dismiss the negative, only receive the positive.

As we approach the moments in our lives that provide options and choices for us, we must accept some things and dismiss others as we move forward. Seeking new information is part of the journey toward trying new ideas and releasing some as well.

Step forward, keeping what works and releasing what doesn't. If we accept what aligns with us, we can let go of what doesn't serve us or others anymore. We begin to pave our way and design a bridge to the hopes and dreams in our life. You are empowered to respond with honor and respect. You are able to hear with no judgement yet choose to not make it a hurdle in your life.

What will you accept and what will you dismiss in your life to take another step?

Here's your chance to create an affirmation of strength.
I accept my _____ to dismiss_____.

After you accept what works or aligns with your soul, dismiss that which doesn't. It shifts your perception. Now we step forward into affirmation number two.

I perceive _____ to believe _____.

What can you perceive differently to believe a new view? What can you perceive to believe in your life to make a shift in your perspective?

Perception is paramount in our view of self, situations, and others. Shifting how we perceive things begins with how you view yourself. Just as young children learn about their own concept of self and their first I AM's, we continue that process every day through life. What changes this perception? Trauma, tragedy, loss, negative individuals, situations, and environments can impact us greatly. If we choose to receive this information and accept it as truth, we inevitably create a new self, one of lack and sometimes even fear.

When we believe negative perceptions and negative beliefs, we bring forth the same in our lives. Yes, the law of attraction and energy is alive and well. We don't embrace our "heart song." What do you want to believe differently? Believing differently will bring forth newness in life and attract what is wanted instead of not wanted.

Your affirmation is to stand in inner power. Choose a new you in life.
I perceive _____ so I can believe _____.
I AM _____. I AM enough!

Compassion is the connection to LOVE. Begin with having compassion for yourself. When love is the focus, you move forward. When fear is, you freeze, flee, or fight, which is not conducive to positive forward movement. Fear promotes stepping "off the path" or "off-roading."

What do you want to believe? Here is your choice to shift your affirmation to…

I PERCEIVE _____ so I can BELIEVE _____.
I AM _____. I AM ENOUGH!

When we can embrace the concept that love is greater than fear, we will see ourselves, each other, our communities, and our world in a more beautiful way. If we focus on our true selves, we will make more conscious commitments emerging from love, abundance, truth, and open-mindedness. We can be heart-driven to honor personal desire, thrive in life, be faith-focused, and stay in connection. Life can be different for all of us. You may locate and follow the truth OR believe the fear. Remember, the choice is always yours.

> *"The opposite of love is not hate, it is fear."*
> —Gary Zukov

Stepping forward requires releasing previous thoughts and beliefs in various areas of life. The physical battleground is where we find the work through the challenge, even though it requires us to engage our hearts and minds. When we allow ourselves to become paralyzed by the fear, we halt our ability to move forward. We believe there is a "tiger" even when there is not. We can even convince others in the threat, just by connecting at the emotional level. Judgement is fear based, and something we have all probably experienced throughout our life. The damage that judgement makes is felt deeply in our hearts, minds, spirits, and overall being. We all carry anchors of judgement from being teased as a child for some small difference or uniqueness. You may have even felt it in the corporate world, organizations, and even communities where others search for power and even low self-esteem resulted in harmful words and actions. The only way to disconnect anchors of judgement is through realizing love is the freedom we all desire. Radiating love is the best defense and the best offense.

What does this look like? The visual analogy I love to use to illustrate it best is swimming.

I LOVE to swim and be near water as much as I can. As I have shared, I'm a beach girl at heart and barefoot or flip flops are my go-to relaxation choices. When I was very ill and healing, my doctors recommended I swim or walk in the water. It was low impact yet had the ability to give me some resistance without increasing pain. Swimming stimulates all of our bodily systems while continuing to nurture it with each movement. When the water is still, swimming is easy and effortless. Pushing the water away from us is not needed because the water feels the weight of the body simply moves out of the way. Yet, when there are waves, current, or wind, the water seems to create resistance and the body struggles. More energy is required to perform the same simple movement. It's similar to life. The more challenges placed in the way, the more the body, mind, heart, and soul struggle.

Some days we may feel like we are treading water, not moving forward in any direction. After a while, treading water requires an energy that becomes so heavy it is difficult to continue. When we float, we decrease the resistance and the water supports us. It is the ability of the body in life to be still and know we are safe and ready with renewed energies when the time is right to embrace what is coming next.

Can you see these examples in your own life? What struggles are in the way of you stepping forward? Do you see them as life preservers or as crashing waves drowning you? Can you float for a moment amid the challenge? Can you refocus and release whatever fear is in the way and receive the safety of what is there for you? A forward focus is required.

Forward Focused

Walking forward requires keeping our eyes on where we are going yet cautiously stepping on the ground underneath us. Taking moments to pause to catch our breath is inevitable and recommended. Pacing our steps for the long walk requires attention to our flow and timing, walking partners, and opportunities.

Flow and the concept of time are integral parts of the journey. When we establish and maintain breath in between our steps, we realize the need for space and quiet to give silence a chance to fill our minds, bodies, and spirits. Life can feel like a race in many ways, so we find our cadence, breath, stamina to keep moving. Staying in our own "lane" is an important concept in our forward positive path.

Bless—Bless not Win—Win

As you walk further forward, you will find some individuals in your life will walk with you. Some will walk ahead of you or even right behind you, and some will not understand where you are walking and walk away from you. Knowing each person we encounter is an integral part of the journey, positively and negatively, we can then embrace the blessings of the lesson our relationship provides.

In many situations in my career and life, I have engaged in joint ventures, collaborations, and even successful partnerships when the interaction and connection blessed all involved. The standard in the past for each of us has been on how to create a "win" for ourselves and a "win" for whoever else is involved. I always felt a focus on how we can "win" is an ego-stimulated concept with an energy pull or "take" aspect instead of a mutual concept with an energy shared and given.

I began implementing a strategy which supported my belief in honoring each other's gifts called "Bless-Bless." As long as the focus of your communication and actions together is on blessing the other person, you will feel the synergy grow and develop. I have shared this concept with many clients and colleagues, and it has been implemented in numerous situations from marriages, friendships, work environments, and community relations. To establish these "bless-bless" connections, you must take the time to share your own needs and intentions for the relationship to begin syncing. Your own gifts must be acknowledged and openly shared, without judgment or fear in any way.

If you follow the "I share, you share, we share" mantra, you will deepen your ability to honor and respect each other. Trust, responsibility, and accountability of actions, language, and feelings will all be part of the steps you take and must be established early in your "walk" together. This is a heartfelt, heart-driven, and heart-led approach. Invest wisely and don't take the signs of challenge lightly either. If something doesn't feel in sync, make sure you are openly communicating. This is an active way of troubleshooting when someone in the process is experiencing difficulty and may be rectified quickly. However, there will be times we walk away on different roads from relationships that can no longer be a "bless-bless" in our lives.

As I shared previously, my work with Dr. Kathryn Cramer and Hank Wasiak, authors of *Change the Way You See Everything* and the ABT psychology, was truly a "bless-bless" relationship. I was honored for over six years to work with Kathy in bringing to life ABT in new situations and environments. The programs we created were a mission of love and commitment to our joint gifts and insights. I learned some of the greatest lessons from her, as well as a deep friendship we had established. Dedicating this book to Kathy was very important to me. She always supported me in knowing who I was and embracing who I was evolving to be. Our work together wasn't without tremendous hurdles, yet our conversations were based on challenge resolution, not accusations and "win-win" mentality. Bless-bless was our motto and we worked diligently to maintain it.

You will find many ways to use "bless-bless" in your life with family, friends, and colleagues. Giving to someone the best of us is the most cherished gift we can offer. What are bless-bless opportunities and relationships you can see in your life right now? Which ones can you shift to be more focused on gifts and blessings?

Time and Flow

Are you a person for whom time is of the essence and are always on time or early for everything? Does time not matter and whatever task or experience or even person you are with at the moment is more important than being early or late? Do you carry guilt about time?

Time eludes us daily. We struggle with its restrictions on us, or we appreciate the protection and security it provides. The more we learn about the spiritual and scientific nature of time, the more we try to embrace the ebb and flow of it. When I received my awareness experience, or "divine download" as I call it, with God and the Universe's expansive concepts, time and flow were an integral part of the conversation. I would like to introduce you to a few of the necessary understandings we must embrace to step forward in our purpose.

Why does it always seem time is against us in life? We either have too much time on our hands and complain about having nothing to do, or we never have enough and can't seem to get everything done. We are either frequently late and seem to place everything we need to do too close together or we are consistently early and bothered when people aren't ready in the same way. Notice the "either/or" absolute concept of time.

As I heard the words in my "divine download" experience, the focus on TIME and FLOW were spotlighted. I wondered why at that time, yet as I have learned and listened further, the impact became clearer for me. Walking forward and focusing on the steps ahead require us to pay attention to our energy as we experience time and its flow in our lives.

Time is a flow of energy and when we are aligned with it and honor its structure, we embrace its passing. Our involvement in how it moves is what we have the ability to control and make choices accordingly. When I was able to comprehend the scope of time and flow, life began to take on a new level of calm and increased my ability to accept how there is truly a "time for everything." You have heard people even say, "go with the flow." It is more than a seventies mantra. It is about releasing our anchor or "tether" to a restrictive feeling.

Kairos, Chronos, and Krisis are all part of the essence of embracing time and its impact on our lives. Yes, some may have even been Greek gods, but in this situation their message for us is more foundational than their myths and stories. Chronos is the constraint of time as we know it today. Sixty minutes in an hour and the chronological nature of how time passes had to be measured to establish continuity for our day. It gave us a common language based on time passing and the need to understand it in a consistent manner. We see examples of this in the early native Americans and other tribes around the world, marked time with moons, suns, lengths of day with the first sundial, and years of life with the seasons. We must see time as an ally in keeping things aligned and not restricted.

Just like you, I was a follower of the "time management" theories and our workplace environments provided lots of opportunities to experience this phenomenon. I can remember as a therapeutic educator having a special schedule every day that had to be followed, and most of the time it did not include understanding of the children I was working with who didn't comply with these time constraints. Yes, I was scheduled to have my children to lunch, music therapy, art therapy, and so on by a certain minute in time, let's call it 12:03. If we were not there by 12:03, we were considered late and penalized. I can remember faculty meetings in which the administrator had to discuss how many teachers were late by minutes to some activity and it created a shift in the successful function of the day. Oh, my goodness! Can you imagine? You know, there are only two places the day is organized in these minute-by-minute increments, schools and airports, and we know they don't mean it in the airports. Ha!

As an administrator, I worked on a slightly different way of picking up lunches or having lunch during a time frame designated by the age or need of the students. It was a Kairos method, not a Chronos one. The stress level and expectation were lower and guess what, everyone got to eat!

Kairos is the appointed, crucial, or opportune time for something to occur. This is God's timing in action. The heightened feeling of being aware is created in the moment as if to say, watch, wait, and grasp its importance. It may be an intersection or a turn in the path toward something you will miss if you are not aware. Synchronicity is an example of Kairos and when recognized and embraced, it can be a source of solution in opportunities as they present themselves.

Krisis is the Greek word for something we are very familiar in our lives. It obviously translates into "crisis." A crisis is only a challenge in which a lesson will be experienced and the learning toward a new or established strength to be gained. It is the moment that creates friction or misalignment between what's previous in life and what is coming next. It is felt and a challenge or opportunity results from it. When these experiences are viewed as a turning point or an opportunity to make a decision, we continue to move forward. When we see time and crisis with fear, we freeze, or we run away from the moments that could have been a breakthrough for us. As you may have had happen, they will come around again with stronger challenge and a deeper lesson will be learned.

Time is important if we embrace the relevancy of its effects. Walking with purposeful expectation and excitement creates a pathway for lessons to be embraced, not feared, and time to be respected, not restricted. Time is not a punishment but a transition to what's coming next. The transition part is what we miss. It is the bridge we use to cross over from being "in the meantime" or "not really wanting to be here in this moment" to "woohoo look at where I am" and "can I stay here and experience this."

I recommend a transition "bubble" when you are in need of making a conscious choice on something in life and require a space to breathe, feel, and prepare yourself for movement.

Besides the aspect of transition, another gentle guiding, comfort feeling period of time is "flow." It is the breath of bliss in action. What experiences do you engage in where you lose complete track of time?

The deeper you are concentrating and enjoying the activity, the faster time seems to pass. For me, it is when I am writing or creating something, being with people I love, playing with my grandchildren, traveling with my husband, or walking on a beach.

Flow is the nature of our efforts felt in our motivation. The "father" of flow is Mihaly Csikszentmihalyi and he explains flow as, "the state which people are so involved in an activity that nothing else seems to matter; the experience itself is so enjoyable that people will do it even at great cost, for the sheer sake of doing it..." Stepping forward requires us to be in motion, motivated, and feeling like we can continue this effort even regardless of time. Being in flow creates longer engagement in an activity to feel our comfort and joy more deeply.

For years I have been fascinated by the concepts of time and energy. In my workshops, I have shared strategies around these concepts. Recently, I shared their implications on our "soul-based" journey and how each component may be acknowledged and honored each day in a more positive and active life. Some of the participants even suggested adding it to the way we ignite our intention each day and as a springboard in meditation and prayer. Powerful considerations! We must see time as shifts in the energy of our day as we create spaces: spaces for breath, silence, love, self, and others. It is more about understanding and appreciating the structure of time, which Chronos gives us, embracing the moments of Kairos as we allow our lives to unfold with purpose, and see the experiences that Krisis brings for us to strengthen and accept the awakening occurring. It is an invitation to throw off old self, chains, and all things that keep me from growing. In essence, Krisis is an opportunity to become free and more true self. Wow! When you can open up to this ease, you will find you can accomplish much more and feel the balance and bliss in everything.

Where do you see time and flow evident in your life? How does this new insight or understanding impact or influence the "be and do" of your daily routine?

Opportunities

Visions and opportunities come in all different shapes and sizes. Sometimes the original vision that started your path to a new endeavor or "mighty cause" reaches a phase of stagnation and change. The one thing I have learned is each stage in the process to "becoming" is patience and reflection.

While going through one of these seasons, a personal business and leadership coach helped me see my struggle and need for a new focus. She provided me insight in the form of a metaphor about a hermit crab. I have elaborated the story and share it often.

If you know anything about this small creature, they undergo changes in their lives, just as we do. Her example gave me the ability to see my vision and reactions to my current situation with more clarity. Just as the hermit crab, I was embarking on a journey of change through three different phases.

Take your time and reflect during each stage of the process. The new insights you gain during the journey ahead will be worth the energy and effort you choose to invest. Honor each step. Think of these stages and ask yourself the corresponding questions provided:

- ♥ **The "Cramped Condo":** This stage is one of awareness and knowledge in your current situation with a focus on the future. Your "shell" is uncomfortable and you need more space and new opportunities so you can continue to grow and develop. *Do I have enough faith and courage to move out of the limiting boundaries of the smaller vision?*
- ♥ **The "Room with a View":** This stage provides time to create a new vision or enhance your current one. You will be shedding your exoskeleton and reflecting on what's working and what skills and talents are necessary to move forward. You will experience limited movement and may feel like you are digging yourself deep into the sand for safety and protection as you prepare for your new phase. *Am I feeling exposed to all? Am I being still in the moment to rest, renew, and shed the old in order to generate the growth necessary to accomplish the new vision coming? Am I ready and equipped for what I have envisioned?*
- ♥ **The "Castle":** This stage encourages the application of all you have learned and envisioned. You are ready for new challenges—ready to grow into your new purpose. You are walking into your vision—you can move freely again with more security and curiosity. You are embracing the quest for a new shell, a bigger dream, a larger task, and greater responsibility. *Is this the "right" opportunity, the most important one, and the vision designed especially for me? Can I carry this shell and grow into its new intended purpose?*

What stage is your vision? Are you ready to accept the challenges and actions required to experience new growth and development? Just as the hermit crab, you must take time at each step of the journey to reflect and bring the wisdom from prior experiences with you. Where are you in the "shell game"?

> *"It is the set of the sails,*
> *not the direction of the wind,*
> *that determines which way we will go."*
> —Jim Rohn

Bound to Boundaries

Why are we discussing boundaries? As we continue to step forward, we need to be prepared for positive boundaries with individuals in our work and life. Have you ever wondered if boundaries are for keeping people out or in? Are they for making us feel safe or for making others feel safe?

A healthy and functional boundary is mutual-respect-focused, multidimensional, and nonphysical in nature, which protects all involved. It is not about building a wall between self and others, but a self-supportive system of maintaining each person's knowledge, truth, and gifts. It is created as a mutually agreed "bubble" of belief that is shared and one that will ensure a positive connection.

How do you use boundaries and when? If activated well, healthy boundaries are a way to practice self-care and respect of others and their gifts. There may be times both cannot happen when others are not ready to establish the parameters for themselves, therefore, one individual may choose to place a boundary to protect and maintain the effort in the relationship. If they are used to respecting each other and ourselves, it is helpful. If they are to shield us from others and keep us in our comfort zone, they are not positive.

Our world has been driven by learning to accept difference. We must embrace these differences by seeing and appreciating how we believe, see, act, and feel in our own way. When we focus on what is working, what is true, what is right in our relationships, we see shifts occur. All characteristics we encounter can be observed and categorized as positive or negative based on our own relationship to those characteristics. For instance, if we had a parent who was overly confident and charismatic, we may view those traits as negative.

Boundaries may have to be strengthened and a type of "filter" put into place when someone chooses not to be supportive in your life. You may love and care about someone, yet not be anchored to them or to their actions. You make a decision to cultivate positive energy to be shared between you both.

Energy, when it is mutually shared, increases in its outreach through positive emotion and action. You feel it. It pulls you to each other and finds us interacting in a closer manner. As women, we are consistently looking for relationships and sisterhood without drama and true friendships with mutual understanding and support.

Releasing our own intentions and connections to individuals who engage or even perpetuate negativity. Yet, forgiving and sending them compassion and kindness raises the energy to a higher level for all people involved. Knowing when to honor yourself and who you are becoming is claiming the personal power from the lesson or experience. It is just a matter of moving on in a new and different direction.

Have you ever watched young children playing in a sandbox? I still love playing with my grandson in the sand and water table. Digging, scooping, smoothing, raking, and creating interactions between toys comes alive. When you are creating boundaries in your life, you are engaging in sandbox play. Children's play has stages of development, just like healthy boundaries. I use the analogy of a neutral sandbox with clients in relationships to provide a visual in how we establish healthy boundaries of respect, cooperation, and intention.

Boundaries, as we step forward, will appear in our ever-changing relationships and responsibilities. Paying close attention to those changes may preempt any unforeseen challenges as you move forward. Boundaries require compassion and supportive statements as you are in the nurturing phase. Usually I choose to focus only on the positive with language and actions, yet the "do nots" in boundaries are powerful.

- ♥ <u>Don't Dismiss</u> the need for a boundary in any relationship or experience. It gives us positive behaviors and parameters to freely function in a positive manner as we honor each person involved.
- ♥ <u>Don't Doubt</u> your feelings or intuition when something or someone has placed you in an uncomfortable situation. Evoke your boundary when necessary.
- ♥ <u>Don't Deflect</u> the emotions you are feeling. Share the truth involved in the relationship to avoid deterioration of the boundaries and the positive platform it is based on.
- ♥ <u>Don't Damage</u> the friendship or relationship with judgement or choosing language with a negative focus.
- ♥ <u>Don't Dismiss</u> your needs or intentions set forth when the relationship or experience was formed. It is important to continue to revisit the shifts and changes as growth occurs as boundaries may need to be adjusted.

Envision yourself and another person with whom you are working on boundaries standing in a room with hula hoops affixed around each of your waists. The hula hoops are filled with your own respective knowledge, insights, feelings, experiences, and desires. You can bump into each other and overlap periodically, but you never drop your hoop or take the other person's. Now translate that into action for yourself. We each own our lessons and they own theirs. Relationships are part of the lessons in life we have chosen. We all desire community and need to learn how to honor each other in life. Relationships are part of our past and our future. They teach us what we need to learn about ourselves. Our voices are needed in harmony, not dissonance.

Understanding boundaries is an integral part of walking forward with purpose. Have you ever refused or chosen to walk into something new and different because a friend told you not to or wouldn't walk with you? Will you choose to walk into your purpose and accept an opportunity even if a friend isn't coming with you?

Sharing part of "housewife" Stephanie's struggle with "best friend" Brandi was only a snapshot of what occurred, as you know. I was so elated that they were able to respect each other's boundaries and establish a new and better relationship, stronger than ever. When they took those first steps, both of them tiptoed forward just a little. They were careful with how each other was feeling and what they were thinking. Stephanie even would talk about being more aware and discerning in taking opportunities offered to make sure Brandi felt good about her decisions as it could affect their friendship. Walking slowly and respectfully is how to reconnect the alignment in your steps together with someone. Valuing their input and ideas is important when you have decided they are a powerful part of your journey. All along, make sure the relationship is leading you both forward, not draining or stopping either of you from becoming who you are meant to be.

Sometimes the decision is different. There are relationships we have all faced that result in someone walking away instead of walking with us. Endings and changes are a predictable part of life. The question will never be whether an ending or a shift will happen, but when it will happen. Author Dr. Henry Cloud in his book *Necessary Endings* shares this powerful quote in regard to relationships and life.

> "In your business and perhaps your life, the tomorrow
> that you desire and envision may never come to pass

if you do not end some things you are doing today. Endings are a natural part of the universe and your life and business must face them, stagnate, or die... my hope is you will be comfortable and confident in seeing, negotiating, and even celebrating some endings that may be the door to the future even brighter than ever imagined."

As Dr. Cloud consistently adds in his workshops and lectures, "sometimes the good cannot begin until the bad ends." Yes, that is a "mic drop moment!"

In Stepping Forward, you will discover your true self and newly developed stamina and endurance as you are trailblazing the path of purpose. Remember the importance of steps? Find your baby steps and tiptoe forward. Inertia becomes momentum. Allow it to shift you forward without the push and pull. Give up the resistance and create a vibrational alignment to a higher good in your life.

I'm so glad we could discuss the important pieces that support us as we walk forward on our journey. Take a moment and walk with me. We are ready to Envision Leap!

Walk with Lori: Stepping Forward

Stepping Forward requires us to manage many aspects of the physical world each day.

Which ones do you struggle with and how will you create more harmony in your steps?

How will you connect with all aspects of time in order to engage in the flow of life?

What stage is your journey of change?

chapter six
Envision Leaping

"It turns out our brains are literally hard-wired to perform at their best not when they are negative or even when they are neutral, but when they are positive"
—Happiness Advantage

Introduction

She stood at the top of a cliff and gazed down below at the turquoise water flowing gently below. As she looked across to the other side, she saw the ground she wanted to safely land on and walk. Was it possible? Did she dare try to place the glider on her back and release her feet from where she was now? She thought about all the possibilities and opportunities to experience on the other side, as she sighed with anticipation and excitement. Reflecting on where she had been and the lessons she had experienced, she said to herself, "Wow, what a journey!" Was she ready to leave the comfort of what she knew to walk into that which she didn't know? She needed the decision now. The chance was here, and the timing was right. Did she leap? What would you do? Are you in this same situation in your life right now? Is it time?

When we leap forward with purpose and passion, we create

an inspired action of intent in our life. We have led up to this moment and appreciate the lessons we've learned and the new I AM's we have accepted with the hope of seeing a glimmer of what is coming. That is what I call Envision Leaping! Think about the last time you took a courageous and large step into something that focused on a life decision or life-altering choice. What led you into action? How did you feel, inspired or terrified?

When we envision our life, we create movement and action through inspiration of what could happen or the "what-if's" in our future. It brings moments of hope and contemplation. It is not a fearful act, as if we would run away or flee from something in our leaping. It also isn't where all the answers will lie without struggle or challenge involved. Yet, it is a new beginning we will engage in as we embrace excitement and fulfillment in our path of purpose.

One of my most memorable moments in *Envision Leaping* focused around my decision in whether to apply to the next level of education in my field, the PhD. I loved what I was doing as a therapeutic educator and educational consultant. Making a difference in the lives of others was still my passion, and I experienced it in numerous ways. I wasn't bored in my positions or ready to move on, but I knew I was being drawn to greater platforms and knowledge was a key component to my outreach. What did I do? I called a very good friend and colleague who I did speaking work with across the state. I trusted her insight, and she had just finished her PhD journey. Who better to ask about my own? She had left her position in an educational environment to pursue her doctorate and leaped into new opportunities to support families and professionals at a higher level with her own message and research. I could see my own path aligning with hers. She knew this road and the steps I would have to take. The illustration she shared has remained with me today and I even use it in my own practice.

When I asked her the question of how I should start my

journey to the PhD, she stated very simply, "Be a KITE." What...be a KITE? What kind of advice was that? What does a kite have to do with making one of the greatest decisions in my life and career? In her quiet and funny wisdom, she stated again, "It is simple, Lori. Just be a kite." The analogy was powerful and so was her insight. How does a kite soar to the highest of heights? It leans INTO the air and catches the breeze of the moment as it floats with a light tether to someone who is guiding its direction. I was so surprised. Be a kite? What a wonderful way to envision the movement I needed to have as I stepped out into the unknown and its possibilities. Her profound nature spoke in such a way to illuminate the path I would follow and I knew through her words that I could do this I would lean IN and float to see new views. Lean IN, and let the wind of change envelop my inner belief in going forward. Yes, I knew I could. That was her hope and intention all along. Thank you, my dear friend, Dr. Becky Bailey, for your words of wisdom just when I needed them.

In this chapter, you will be reading short concepts to remember as you envision your leaping forward. Each of these are simple motivations to illumine your path, especially into the greatest challenge of bridge building into the unknown, dreaming big enough to scare you, and designing the ANDs in your life. We will be revisiting how to ignite intention in these experiences, how letting go is a part of the process, and where forgiveness becomes extensively involved. So let's "dance and leap!"

Dancing and Leaping to Texas...Boots and All

Envision leaping became part of my life in many different aspects and especially in my decision to move to Texas. As I have shared in Chapter 4, my move to Texas was filled with chaos and clarity, drastic hurdles and memorable highlights, the largest being meeting and marrying my best friend, Art. Once grounded in the culture and community of Dallas and Fort Worth, I leaped further in my boots to becoming part of it. Encountering all that was new, I deeply placed my roots into the soil and allowed my mind, body, and spirit to be nurtured and enhanced by the environments and relationships around me. You know how I love shoes, too! Well, you should see my turquoise cowboy boots! They are ready, willing, and able to dance or walk further as needed.

Did I miss my home in Florida, my friends and family, as well as the memories there? Of course, I went back frequently. To this day the minute the plane lands or the car pulls over the state line, I take a breath of air that just feels familiar and more like home. Did I experience challenge and crisis in my leap? Of course! Each one of them became new lessons and opportunities for me to become who I AM today and who I AM becoming tomorrow. Will I envision leap again? What do you think?

Are you ready to envision leap in your life? Maybe you would be more ready to build a bridge first.

Bridges on the Journey

In some circumstances of life, we are not able to or have time for envision leaping. Bridges provide passage across one piece of our experience onto a new uncharted one. Building a bridge, finding ourselves on a bridge, and being a bridge are all part of the adventure.

Building a bridge is a step-by-step process with clarity, conviction, and commitment. It begins with *Igniting Intention* as we have discussed earlier in Chapter 4. But now, you have been walking this path forward for a while, and the intentions are a daily routine in your life. As we say, you wouldn't go anywhere without them. You will be igniting your intentions with more fervor and persistence, stronger vision and purpose, and feel guided and directed in your steps.

Your new I AM is a warrior woman and shall we say, goddess of goodness. Remember, be a **warrior woman** (movement manifested, action-oriented, and DO-focused) and a **goodness goddess** (wisdom and intention, reflection and realization, and BE-focused) as you reach through the moments of change for balance and bliss, courage, and confidence in your life. Wear your armor and sword proudly when needed, but be ready to put on your flowing spirit and inviting glow, too. Step forward on the boards safely attached to structures of support across the ravine. You want to keep your eyes forward with a gaze upward, not down where difficulties and challenges lie. When we look down we see the absence of what we may feel should be the foundation beneath us or what we have known; we realize we may be alone on this path. The risk is only in the steps we take. The truth and belief rest in the brilliance of THE Architect and Creator God in life. Release your connections and anchors to those who won't cross the bridge with you. The path will present itself as you trust, hope, and love those who are blessings in each step.

Think of the igniting intention steps in Chapter 4 to guide your way. Why I term this stage *Envision Leaping* is because the first step in intention is **ENVISION**. You are balancing your BE and DO simultaneously. Your I AM's are part of the process. Your bridge will be designed just for YOU...the YOU now and the new YOU blossoming on the journey.

I am...
I will...
I wonder...
I dedicate...

One of the most important questions I ask in this building process is, "are you ready for this step?" This is all part of the BEING before you are DOING. Ask yourself, "Am I ready?"

Our next step is **RELEASE**. It is time to *RELEASE to RECEIVE* the bridge being created to ensure you are envisioning before leaping. Let go of those anchors and areas of resistance that no longer serve you. You can say, "What will I release to receive? Am I ready to release as well as ready to receive? If not, what will I do to become ready?"

How will you **MANIFEST**? Manifesting is the allowing and acceptance of gifts and abundance along the way. How will you share in the creation of the bridge? How will you assist the Creator in the design? Where will your gifts be needed? What steps do you need to take to embrace the abundance being provided? Ask yourself again, "Am I ready?"

The last and most important step is **RECEIVE**. Ask yourself, how will I receive the blessings of this bridge in my journey? How will I share my wisdom and experience on the bridge with others to support their steps? What is gratitude for me in this moment? Lastly, ask yourself, "am I ready?"

Cary, during Season 2, stood her ground and shared with Mark how she loved being a mom and being a nurse. Mark felt concerned for her as she was choosing to walk across a new bridge in her life, without him. They do so much together in their lives and clinical practice, yet this was somewhere he couldn't go with her. She needed to do this walk on her own. New, improved, and empowered, Cary was ready for the challenge. It took the summer to make adjustments and for Cary to find her rhythm in her roles and her independence, too. Stepping out, as we know, is the most difficult part of the journey.

Once you are in motion, the stepping up and forward is to achieve one step at a time and that's what she was doing. As we see in the first episode of the new Season 3 of RHOD, Cary has created her flow and used the essence of time to work for her. It wasn't about a day here, a day, there, but rituals. She loved waking Zuri up, having snuggle time, making breakfast, and enjoying the morning together. Then, Cary was ready to go on to work and take Zuri to school or play time. What a perfect solution! Mark was thrilled to have Cary back and they designed a practice for her to do Botox and other injectables, as well as laser, and have her own clients. It was the best of both worlds and a perfect option for an empowered woman! As Cary states in episode 1, "I'm a 'boss bitch' now." Own it, girl! The bridge was in place, and they crossed over successfully into new territory together.

What bridge are you beginning to envision?

Building a bridge isn't for everyone. Sometimes you find yourself reacting to a bridge that has been given to you. If you remember in Season 2 of RHOD, Stephanie and Travis, or shall we say Travis, decided to bid on a home online. They had been talking about moving closer to the boys' schools and to friends in the Dallas area. But Travis thought it would be fun to bid on a mansion valued at over $13 million in an elite section of Dallas. Never thinking they would receive the winning bid, he shared what he did with Stephanie. Guess what her reaction was? Yes. It was one of shock and disbelief. She actually thought he was kidding! The home was overwhelmingly large and had a pool in the entryway as a focal point to the entire home. So, what happened? If you didn't see for yourself, they won the bid! Had they decided to build a bridge? No, they found themselves standing on a bridge and one needing immediate attention in many ways.

You may ask yourself, how did I get here? Standing on the bridge may bring up feelings of fear and vulnerability. There is nothing underneath you, and sometimes you can't walk backwards to comfortable and familiar steps. You may feel like you are reinventing yourself, yet in reality you are creating your new I AM for what is now and what is coming. It requires learning to be comfortable in the uncomfortable. Using balance and bliss while learning to BE more than DO, is your life line. There is always more progress in the difficult than the familiar. As you feel it and embrace the process, you become relaxed and accept it going forward.

While you are standing on the bridge, continue to ignite your intentions. First, Stephanie and Travis visited their new opportunity and gathered information together. Carefully listening and taking in what the other person was excited about and challenged in at the same time is key. Then, they began brainstorming solutions and options. Would they live there? Was it family friendly? What does it need? Next, Stephanie examined her feelings about the house and decided what she needed to feel comfortable in living there. Finally, they acknowledged where they were on the bridge, the choices it offered them, and the decisions they needed to make. What did they do? They moved forward one step and contemplated the next one, eventually finding themselves in the new adventure. What a journey it was!

Bridges are there to teach us lessons and help us grow. They are there for new opportunities and to experience challenge, too. The result of not envisioning your path is stagnation. When we do not have purpose moving forward, we become paralyzed, and fear becomes the lens through which we see ourselves and the bridge.

As she has shared so bravely in a public forum, Stephanie has experienced depression, and I witnessed its result firsthand as we were working through her relationship challenges with Brandi last year. Season 3 of RHOD, which has just kicked off as I write these last chapters, will be sharing Stephanie's battle with depression. Depression is when we feel in lack, then in fear, we allow paralysis to enter our minds, bodies, and spirits. It results in sadness and the inability to see our life moving forward. We cannot problem solve or see the happiness and blessings all around us, even when they are everywhere. I am so proud of her for being willing to share this deeper side of her life. Her message can help in elevating the discussion around depression and hopefully bring more resources and solutions to others.

For this very reason, it was important to Stephanie and Travis to brainstorm and visualize the "what-if's" in their purchase of a new home. As an empowered woman, it was equally as important to be part of the decision-making process and the renovation, too. In our conversations together, she continued to see the opportunities and possibilities on the bridge and the new "land" on the other side of it.

Building a bridge sometimes isn't an option, though. But being the bridge for others and responding to the bridge IS. As I have walked forward in my new journey, I have shared my calling with you. Being a bridge for others is all part of everyone's life. You may become the conduit or guide to others walking across with you into a new part of their life or yours. Are you ready to accept the challenge? Listen to God in those moments, and you will know when, why, then move toward allowing the how.

As we begin to look at how we can dream big, there is one caution or reminder about how bridges work when we envision leap. Make sure you are balancing your ability to "BE" in life as much as you are connecting to the "DO." You want your bridge to be over triumphant waters, not troubled waters.

DREAM BIG

Dreams shift our thoughts to ones of hope and opportunity, while tapping into the creative side of mind where anything can happen. Dreams are powerful and filled with vision and possibility, which brings our desires into a real space of creation. They encourage us to stretch forward, imagine more broadly, and be impacted by connections and interactions we have in our lives.

When we open up the view wider and adjust the lens to see

the dream in full color and intensity, our eyes shift to witness these vivid images. I see our dreams as bubbles floating around us. They are activated by just one breath of positive intention, soaring from our past and present into our future. They flow in an energetic path of color and light inspiring us to keep moving forward and not let go.

In my previous career as a speaker, I was known as the "bubble lady. When I traveled across different states, many times by car, I would carry bubbles in my center console. When I was stuck in traffic, I would sit and blow bubbles, usually out of my convertible or sunroof openings. I used bubbles a lot in my therapeutic classrooms since breathing for children and youth with anxiety or attentional challenges was incredibly calming. You have to admit, you love them, or you did at one time in your life. Now, as a nana, we always have bubbles available.

During one of these bubbles blowing sessions with adults, I saw the beautiful room filling up with iridescent little globes of breath. The sunlight in our environment was creating this gorgeous view, and I realized these little spheres contained not only a breath, but a thought, a moment, during our work together. For some people in the learning session, it was a "press pause" moment. For others it stimulated great thought, and for others it unleashed calmness and a download minute of the intense connections they were making. For me, they became "dream bubbles." Recently, God reminded me to bring back this concept just for you.

These "dream bubbles" of breath are filled with one memory, just enough of a "spoonful" for us to release and focus. They are bubbles of protection, positive based, and more than a heart string memory of ours. They have powerful purpose, a moment you want to remember that applies to your dream moving forward. They are past and present focused and may be a dream you could never let go of in your life. Some dream bubbles are a moment in time we want to experience over and over and over again when we need it most. They can be those moments that take our breath away or make us sigh deeply. They fuel us to walk forward on our dream path in a big way. Can you see them? What are in your dream bubbles? Let them float filled with possibility toward the opening of your purpose. Can you feel yourself dreaming? Now dream BIGGER!

Why does dreaming BIG scare us? Cynthia, a dear client, was aware of all the passions in her life and was walking boldly in some of the areas she was called to engage her talents and gifts. Her mission was beautiful, yet the scope of the dream was only what she could see, feel, hear, and touch. Could she dream bigger? That was the task we tackled together. Stretching so far and seeing those dream bubbles around us as they drift upward or in front of us effortlessly, is a step in the process. Cynthia would dream so big it freaked her out, then we would let the greatness of God carry her further into her purpose. Her daily intentions were set, and manifesting was happening. I could see just enough in front of her to know it was a breathtaking view. She began to float and walk in her new dreams, brilliantly embracing them with excitement and anticipation. I love how the author and leader James Maxwell shares, "dream big enough for God to rush inside and perform His miracles for you." It only leads us further along in the process to feel confident to *Envision* life and *Leap* with purpose.

Ask yourself, "will I walk, will I fly, will I leap into what's next in my life?" Sometimes we walk. Sometimes we fly. Sometimes…we just LEAP!

Either/OR? Or…ANDs

Dreaming BIG entices us to bring in the ANDs of our life in order to step forward and LEAP. Do you know what the ampersand or "and" sign truly means as we walk with determination in life? I love one of the meanings behind the ampersand in the tattoo designs people wear. It symbolizes an attachment to something or someone, or it can represent an endless journey or quest. We are all on an endless journey, and when we pursue the ANDs in life, we explore life's potential.

Life is made up of "ands" more than it is comprised of an either/or options. Moving forward is challenging, but envision leaping can be even more difficult for us. Sometimes you know it is time; even though you may not want to move on, the journey is providing a leap into a new path. Recently, I was stepping down from a very important women's organization I had been the "blessed co-founder" for almost three years. As a co-founder and originator of the organization, my colleague and I stepped hand in hand, arm in arm, to create monthly events, workshops, materials, and retreats. We loved feeding and facilitating our women to not network, but to learn to connect with the "heart." After you work so closely with someone, you sometimes begin to experience challenges. Eventually, even with our diligent discussions, there were some challenges we couldn't reconcile. Call it creative difference or collaboration collapse. It was evident we needed to work separately and not together any longer. It was a very difficult decision for me. I loved the women in our tribe, yet the work was shifting and my relationship with my friend and colleague was changing. Was it painful? Yes! It was like experiencing a death, and I grieved what we had created together and what I was leaving behind.

I knew God was leading me in a new and determined direction, one which caused me to dream BIG again. I heeded his call

> I believe we are to see and embrace life as a series of new ANDs that give us options, opportunities, and a positive view of moving forward.

to action and stepped down from my responsibilities. I was not walking away from the women, only the program. At the final evening event we would conduct together, I shared my insight of "Either/OR" for women to know, care, and follow both of us with different views and missions in life.

Seeing only either/OR's in life is a very "absolute thinking" model. Making choices in our lives is a necessary and empowering social and emotional skill. Yet, sometimes realizing how to create the positive and powerful "ands" in life is better. How to see life through the lens of acknowledgement in saying, "yes, AND" creates more of a shift than you will ever imagine leading you forward. When you use an either/or statement, you must choose one option over another. It may also give the perception that one choice is better. In my example above, either/or wasn't how we wanted things to be perceived. As empowered adults, we appreciate the ANDs in life. Find yours.

Here are some of my "ands" in life that assist me in my own daily walk in purpose.

- ♥ Balance & Bliss (B & B): Each week I have a day of "balance & bliss" as I have shared with you. Seeing my grandson and spending time with my sweet husband is a powerful way to experience it in action. Watch my Facebook page for even more examples, stories, strategies, and reminders to find your own moments of B&B.
- ♥ Feel and Flourish: A reminder to focus on the feelings, not just the thoughts in the moment, and create ones that will flourish positively for movement forward in your life.
- ♥ Reflect and Renew: Take those quiet moments you have and savor them with reflection on what is powerful and possible. Walk forward with a new sense of renewal.

♥ Know and Own: One of my favorites in life! So many examples to choose from in our life! I ask you, "what will you choose to know and OWN to empower you forward?"

What are some of your ANDs in life? Are you now seeing that the ANDs are necessary when you are preparing for that dream to come to fruition? It's now time for you to fully accept the call! ELEVATE your life. ENVISION it. LEAP into purpose.

Igniting Intention through Releasing

Remember *Release to Receive*? We want to exercise that "muscle" every day. Walk in intention and all the opportunities joy and love with HOPE.

I have been asked, "Is letting go an option? Does letting go mean giving up?"

No. It means you chose YOU...your family, your health, your mission, your journey, your outreach, your_____ (fill in the blank).

Now is the time, the space in this moment to reignite your intention. Choose it. Manifest it You are part of something fabulously outrageous, and we need you. God needs you to bring forth your mission in this world right now. He has ordained you for these steps. Remember how we dedicated our steps in the igniting intention process? Bring this forth in your leaping and dedicate it to yourself, to God, to someone you love, but make it happen.

I love these comments inspired by Dr. Michael Beckwith in his work.

You talk about INTENTION and MANIFESTATION...talk to it. Then, see it everywhere...then you talk from it within yourself. You align to it vibrationally or you lose it. It doesn't become part of you or align with where you are on the journey. Yet, you can energetically radiate and attract it.

When you realize the lessons are there to help us climb and leap higher, you begin to see each day overflowing with intention. Shifting the harm in our lives to glimmers of hope becomes our focus and the view we see in each moment. It allows our words and actions to be from a place of personal POWER and one of strength in knowing and owning the journey and purpose, not a fragile space of uncertainty, questioning, and vulnerability. It is your time to set your spark in life and ignite your intentions.

Two Steps Forward, Three Steps Back...Understanding Our Hurdles and Highlights

Where's your focus? Do you look only at your hurdles and not at your highlights in life? When the good times are here, do you see the blessings or do you only see them in times of struggle? As we have discussed, life is about leaping with vision, yet sometimes we experience the difficulties and drama while in mid-air, which can result in a rough landing. My walk forward in many aspects of life has had its "dance" along the way of two steps forward and three steps back. It is all in how we see those setbacks that will determine our next steps. If you want to embrace the "leaps," you have to be willing to tumble.

I want to share two stories with you, one personal and one about a fabulous woman named Kaaren. My story begins with meeting the love of my life and soulmate, Art. What I haven't shared with you or even with many, is the instant roles we both accepted in our lives, and I don't mean as husband and wife. Art and I are both parents, separately, not jointly. We have always felt that love expands and we try to practice that belief, especially where our children are concerned. We have a beautifully blended family and we each felt deeply about not being "step parents." We have always considered ourselves just "other parents." They are all our kids "in love." Their individual circumstances are very different, and they all live in different places. I have already shared a story about our son, Luke, and our "daughter-in-love," Amanda. This story focuses on my "daughter-in-love," Heather. We are so excited about her life and what her journey is providing for her and others. Let me explain.

Heather is getting married in 2019 and we are very happy about our new "son-in-love to be." He has a sweet daughter, Lilly, and we had already adopted her as our next granddaughter when they all met. She is vivacious, precious, and full of joy. We have all vacationed together as a family and knew they would be a perfect fit, but mostly for Heather. It has created a beautiful love path for her and her new fiancé, and she has accepted the new role as mother for Lilly with so much grace. She doesn't see herself as a "step mom" either and neither does Lilly. Their story is just beginning, and we know it will have success moments but also stumble moments, too. But the beautiful part is she is ready for the cheers and the challenges, and she wants us to come along with her.

I am blessed to have this shift in our relationship to one of "other mother." When we first started our relationship together, Heather and I really got along, yet there were those moments of concern whether I would be a good wife for her dad. Would he be happy? Would I treat him well? Would I welcome her in our home? Yes, we all allow the fears of not being accepted or included to come in. I had those same feelings. Would they like me? Would they think I was good for their dad? Would we all get along? We never stopped appreciating the dance, the willingness to communicate even when difficult, and just love each other through the process. She IS my daughter, and I am very proud of her in the journey she has traveled and can't wait to see where she goes next. We will always be there for her and her new family. That is what loves does…it expands and goes in the crevices of our hearts where we need it most! Without this ability, sometimes life can turn out very differently. I am glad I chose this path. The blessings have been overwhelming. Now to the second story I wanted to share that portrays such a fabulous example of leaping.

I know the most amazing woman I chose to call a friend. Her name is Kaaren and I can't wait to share a piece of her story with you. Kaaren and I met and immediately started sharing insights into life and laughing about the funny things that happen. She had an innate way of showing her faith and belief in all that she did, as well as her hysterical sense of humor. Life was getting ready to really LEAP for her, and we were talking about it frequently as she took her steps into motion. All of a sudden, things were different. She had already purchased a fabulous little storefront on a downtown main street, which would be the new home for her business and passion, hand-dyed yarns. The build-out was to feel like a farmhouse kitchen welcoming everyone to come enjoy their craft together. Kaaren was filled with excitement and anticipation as each area was designed exactly how she envisioned it in her mind. The pivotal point was when she found and purchased a double-sided, stainless-steel, giant commercial sink for herself. Once it was put into place, she knew God was telling her this dream was to be a reality. What she didn't expect was what happened next. Kaaren and her husband had been working on their marriage, and she thought they were on solid ground. Little did she know they would be ending their relationship and she would find herself alone and only a storefront to house her possessions. How could this have occurred?

Going from heartful to hopeful in moments such as these can prove to be impossible for some. Yet, even in tragedy there lies triumph. As we talked through the next steps on her journey, the phrase I kept receiving from God to share with her was, "Everything you need is already at your feet." It felt like a trite statement, but the truth is…it WAS. When she needed something and didn't want to purchase it from somewhere else, it was already there. Sometimes it was as simple as repurposing a piece of furniture that would perfectly fit in a new area. Her new store has become her "home" for not only herself, but a new kitten and will be a "home" for everyone who enters, which was God's intent all along. These are only a few of her stories of possibility and promise as she manifested "everything she needed" for her life. I want to celebrate Kaaren Curtis on her new business, NO ORDINARY YARN, which specializes fresh hand-dyed fibers, fabulous yarns for knitting and crocheting, as well as workshops, necessary supplies, and tools. She will be opening this fall, and you will want to follow her ever-evolving business adventure, online shop, and blog of her escapades. To hear more about her story, you can find her on social media and on her blog by the same name.

In this type of situation, we choose to embrace resistance or release. Obviously, Kaaren chose to release. God has given you a dream of brilliance and magnificence. When you act with resistance, you create the decision to walk away and not receive it. You can feel it in your soul. How do you know you are resisting? This can take a form of self-sabotage, self-judgement, procrastination, or not investing in yourself and your talents. There is good news about resistance, though. It can mean the bigger the resistance you feel or allow, the larger and more meaningful the mission and purpose you have. Kaaren knew this. Choosing to walk forward is the only way you can be who you are meant to be.

Do you still have anchors that you need to release? It is the most powerful work we can understand and strive to overcome. Maybe it is hidden in the masks we wear.

＊＊

The Masks We Wear

You have heard others speak about the "authentic self." It has become the latest buzzword in the discussions about being the real you, what I call your I AM. We can also look deeply at the mask we may place over our I AM in order to relate with others, or so we may think. If we are not careful, the mask becomes more about fear, judgement, and worth, as it attaches itself to our anchors in life. You begin asking yourself, "Will they like the real me?" or "If they really knew who I was, no one would come close." Yet, even though we really want people to like the true us, we only want to share with them the mask we wear.

When we leap with our vision turned fully ON, we need to make sure we are only wearing our truest, most brilliant I AM self. Your vision knows; your purpose knows; and most of all, you know. If you jumped with your mask on, you would end up landing somewhere else like the person in the next example.

I want to share a story about a precocious and gifted little boy, named Austin. He was one of my most endearing little boys and at five years old. He had learned how to observe people, especially adults, and see them for who they truly were. The challenge was, in Austin's defense, he had no problem telling them he saw them, and it wasn't always positive. I met this little insightful child while I was a principal at a school in Florida. It was a small school, kindergarten through fourth grade, and focused on supporting children and their families who may be in categorized as "at risk" for educational difficulties. What a horrible label! Can you believe when we created the school they wanted to name it that? I always called our children and their families...AT HOPE, not AT RISK. I felt it served all of us better. We had very special teachers who were there every day for extended hours dedicating themselves to not only the academic needs, but social, behavioral, health, and any other needs which would arise. We had approximately three hundred children my last year, and they were my joys. We were very cautious to interview and hire only the highly qualified, and the highly "called" due to the challenging nature of our jobs every day. Most of the time, we found just the right fit for just the right position.

In one kindergarten class we hired a teacher named Cindy, and she would become Austin's teacher. Cindy came with a fabulous background that included specialized training and even with all the interviews she had and offers she received, she chose us. We were overjoyed. There was something always a little concerning about her as she began setting up her classroom and her reactions to the rest of the staff, who were quite close. She was welcomed in to their small group, and they were readily available for her whenever she needed them. Something just seemed not quite right. When the students arrived on the first day, she portrayed a very strange reaction.

As they walked into the school, we were all lined up outside cheering them on and giving them high fives and handshakes. They were super excited, and everyone was sharing their own enthusiasm for a fabulous year! Cindy was barely smiling and not comfortable giving the kids or the families the interaction they needed. It was a very noticeable sight. We all just thought it was maybe first year nerves and feeling overwhelmed, but maybe we should have paid closer attention.

It was around the sixth week of school, and there were beginning to be severe concerns. Children were frequently sent to the office, and parents were complaining. She began not welcoming any coaching or support from other personnel and consultants we brought in to assist her in feeling more successful, just like we did with our children.

One morning as the children were getting started on their seatwork in their classroom, Austin was struggling with his. Not with the work itself, he was very ahead for a five year old, but with observing his teacher as she interacted with each child as she walked around their tables behind them. She presented her words of encouragement strangely, and most of the children had learned to ignore her and keep working, since that's what she valued most. You see, as she walked around supporting and praising each child as they worked by saying "thank you for working" and "thank you for being on task," it didn't fit her tone or expression. She should have been noticing what they were doing well and using their names to match each delivery with a particular child. But it was more than that. Her monotone voice and lack of smile was evident. Austin had to say something, and he knew the result of speaking up was that he would be sent to see the principal, me. He took a chance and loudly stated directly to her, "I only wish your words would match your face." Wow! You could hear the other children gasp, then giggle with their heads down. What she didn't know was I was standing at the doorway bringing in a tardy student and heard the entire altercation this time. She immediately started yelling and grabbed him by the back of his shirt, pulled him up to his feet, and began dragging him to the door when her eyes met mine. I quietly removed Austin for the day and let her know we would talk later. He was very ready to accept his discipline and knew what his behavior should have been during that time of the day. But, he shared with me how we truly believed in what he said to her and actually, he was right. Cindy and I spoke later and she never did understand how she needed to reflected upon his message, just how she had been "abused" by a student. We mutually agreed soon after that she was not a good fit for our students, and she moved to a different school.

Have you ever wanted to say to someone, "I wish your words matched your face" or better yet, "your mask"? We all have certain things we share with others and show in different situations. But ask yourself, "Do I let others see the inside of my mask, my true nature?" What do we reveal to others? Is it our "authentic self" or the one we feel most comfortable showing at this time? To envision requires authenticity, and to leap requires even more knowing and owning of who we truly are to be most successful.

Who knows the most real you? Are they someone you can bring with you on the journey? Will you need to move forward without them, or will you design a healthy boundary for their positive participation? Yes, it may be an AND!

With Me? Without Me?

Have you asked yourself, "Who's on the journey with me?" Do you wonder if they are with you, or maybe they have gone on without you? The realization that everyone will not be going over the bridge and moving on with you is inevitable. You may also know you may not join them on their journey, too.

In the movie *Knight and Day,* Tom Cruise says to Cameron Diaz, "Are you with me or without me?" Cruise's character shares the rationale that being with him on this ludicrous adventure would give her more protection and likelihood of safety, than being without him. He repeatedly asks her in many different circumstances the same question, and she finally agrees being "with him" is much safer than trying to manage all of the difficulties without him.

There are those people in our lives who we need "with us," and we may inquire if they are going with us through the darkness to come out into the light. They have their own choices to make too. The same is true for those you may not want to leap into your new vision with you.

Knowing how you feel about the outcome of the questions and how to strategize having them "with you" or "without you" is the ultimate mission to manifest. Will you be ready, willing, and able? How will you prepare? Honoring and embracing the steps you have already taken is a beautiful way to get started. Are you with me?

Honoring and Embracing Your Steps

Remember the comfort zone of my gray slippers and couch days? Well, I learned to embrace those days, and when I revisit them for a few days, it forces me to honor them. My husband is an amazing man and keeps me going in so many ways in life. We both find fun and relaxation in movies, travel, music, and enjoying theme parks, especially Disney. We love to take our grandchildren and meet friends there, and it still takes me back to my first visit when I was five years old and my parents took my sister and me. It was on one of these trips a few years ago where we met friends for a special event at Disney World in Orlando. On this particular trip, Art ordered me a wheelchair so I could still go with everyone. I was mortified. What had happened to me? Was this to be my life going forward? As I shared with you, there was a time I couldn't walk or stand for very long. The wheelchair and a cane were part of my accessories.

Fast forward to a more recent trip where I walked through the gates and remembered being there seeing everything in a wheelchair. As I walked all day, I kept saying, "remember when you pushed me through this…remember when we had to sit there because of my wheelchair." It made a deep impact on me. Honoring and embracing how far I have come and how much I walk every day now is amazing. Do I still baby my knee and back to conserve my energy each day? Yes. But in these positive self-care moments, I am blessed for how far I have come!

Now my family, especially my husband, will say, "you've got this!" Last November, we took our entire family to Disney World, and I knew with each stronger breath, each moment of laughter, each step with braver purpose, I was doing exactly what I should be doing right now. I may be slower sometimes than our teen grandkids or our grown children, but it allows me to savor the moments and see things through different eyes, ones of balance and of bliss.

There is only one more topic for us to share together, and it is one which brings the greatest challenge and the most joy... forgiveness.

Forgiveness

In the process of **Igniting Intention**, we shared the stages and aligned them with your life and daily routine. Gratitude is a major part of the process, and to be truly grateful and thankful, we need to embrace our connection to forgiveness.

Part of moving forward, and especially leaping into life, is letting go. Letting go of the baggage we all carry, the bags of relationships that failed, individuals we feel wronged or hurt us, shame and blame we have felt from circumstances, and feelings of lack and even judgement. We have witnessed their heavy chains holding us in the past from moving on to new opportunities. We have secretively locked them away in the vaults of our heart and soul hoping no one would hear the cries they make.

You have made decisions to Step OUT from the weight of the bags, to Step UP into new choices, and to Step Forward with your talents and gifts showing. Some bags were released, and some are still straggling behind you. As you Envision your Leaping, you clearly see freedom and weightlessness in the ease of your mission. It feels empowering, and all burdens of the past are only a memory behind you. How did you finally let the last few bags, totes, backpacks, and luggage on wheels stay behind? That is the final step in the journey to new life and purpose...forgiveness.

You've heard the words before, "You need to forgive them." Whether it was from a parent, a religious organization, school, or friend, the discussion is still present. Words of "I'm sorry," "please forgive me," "sorry for _____," still exist in our conversations. "Some of you may say, "oh no! I can forgive most people, but not_____." Your freedom is dependent on how you see your life moving on with the toxicity and negativity that this last bag holds for you. You may ask, "Why do I need to forgive them?" or "I did forgive them, but they didn't forgive me and keep punishing me for it." In either instance, you are carrying the weight and it will affect your purpose and your lessons in life going forward.

> *"You must first let go of your past before you can lay a hold of the future God has prepared for you."*
> —Christine Caine

What is forgiveness? It is more than saying, "I'm sorry." It is the flowing of love to someone else without needing it in return. It is more about releasing our self from the anchor or tether of the experience or the person so shame and blame cannot manifest. I believe it is love in action that heals the inward and outward.

My mom was nearing her last few days here with us before transitioning to heaven. We all knew this and everything else in life became secondary to being with her. There were moments where she was speaking and then others when she seemed to be in a perpetual sleep mode. During the lucid moments, she would call for me to be there and began telling me about an experience in our past together. She would then ask for my forgiveness. She knew how important it was to release those past hurts and resentments before moving on. I was blessed to receive her words and asked her for forgiveness in many of the instances, from being a difficult mom sometimes to not understanding my gifts and facing them with fear. Mom now embraced who I was, and we exchanged a deeper love in those face-to-face connections. I am more blessed now to remember those times of sitting by her bedside and honoring her life and what we had together. We started new conversations of how forgiveness gives us the power to love "inverted" in our past to affect our present. We only were grateful in the end for our love and our joy of the journey as mother and daughter.

As you have been reading, practicing igniting intentions in your life, and giving gratitude in all aspects of your life, the amazing power of positive energy is being shared from your soul directly to the soul of others. Forgiving yourself and others is the honoring of love in these actions. The most beautiful form of meditation is the forgiveness prayer as practiced in the Hawaiian culture. HO'OPONOPONO was used by the Hawaiians as an important part of bringing balance, right understanding, and peace of mind to those involved and concerned based on the universal concept of repentance and forgiveness on a person-to-person basis. Yet, it is a practice in every religion and many cultures, too. The belief in forgiveness is part of human nature and desired by the heart of our soul.

"Forgiveness has the power to bring harmony within and with others."
—Jonathon Davis

The Ho'oponopono chant has an updated version with four simple steps: repentance, asking forgiveness, gratitude, and love. It is the powerful words of "I'm sorry" paired with "please forgive me," then offering gratitude in "thank you," and closing in the highest vibrational energy, "love." I am not teaching the use of Ho'oponopono but offering to you its beautiful meaning and as well as the release it provides. You are taking responsibility for actions that have created discord in relationships or episodes in life. Find more about the beautiful process and chant to begin your practice fully. There are beautiful meditations for you to use.

The powerful release the words "I'm sorry" can provide is there for all of us. If you hear it in this way, the meaning deepens and expands. "I realize I am responsible for the challenge in my life and feel saddened and remorseful for something in my consciousness that has caused this. I accept learning from this experience and ask for release from the feelings in moving forward. Resolution is my intention."

My last story in this chapter is about my special relationship with my daughter Maggie. For many years, we have had the blessing of my granddaughter spending the summer with my husband and I. That all came to a halt a couple of years ago and broke our hearts. My daughter and I have a unique bond, and that's a whole book in itself that I will be sharing soon. Our love is a deep, heart-based connection, and we have always been able to feel when we need each other. After having our granddaughter for a few months, there was a misunderstanding between us. It severed our heartstring and created a block we couldn't move, no matter what we said or what heartfelt messages we shared. My husband and I were broken hearted. We grieved the loss of our family and the relationships for not just us but our other kids and grandkids, too. They had chosen not to have any further communication or interaction with my daughter and her family. We were devastated. How could this be mended? My husband doesn't show tears very often even though he feels things deeply in life. We were in church one day and both of us just started crying uncontrollably. They were tears of release and it was in that moment we gave the situation to God, asking for forgiveness for any wrongdoings in our actions and uplifted our entire family to Him for healing. It was through our tears that healing started. The experience wasn't resolved, yet we had peace. We knew one day we would be able to have resolution, and a foundation of a new love were result.

I cannot tell you everything was beautiful and changed immediately, but the peaceful feeling remained. There were many difficulties in the situation which occurred, yet we remained faithful in the process. God works in His timing, remember? Time is all relative in life. Moving forward in love is the expectation. One day I received a strange call from Maggie's husband. She wanted to talk with me, and it was an "emergency." It was the first time in over a year. I was anxious and wondered what could be wrong. She wanted to ask me a question. It was posed very simply, and my heart jumped, "Will you forgive me?" What? Had God answered our prayers? Would she forgive us for anything she felt occurred? The power answers of "YES" on both sides was given. The intense feelings in that moment was felt by all of us. The blame, the shame, the resentments, and pain were being released from the deep anchors in our hearts and soul. It was in that moment we began the new journey to what would be our relationship now.

Can I tell you we are back to being best friends, talking all the time, and the family has healed? No, but our relationship is building a beautiful new trust, and our brief conversations are about the present and the future, not the past. We chose to move forward and not to rehash the past. Healing is in the present and in your next steps on the path. I love her dearly and my granddaughter as well. I continue to pray that one day we will see them and a new blossom will occur. Right now, we are blessed with our conversations, and they know we love them. I chose to celebrate her beautiful life and what she is envisioning in her own leaping moments. I continue to be honored to be her mom and hope she feels the same.

Where do you feel healing needs to occur in a relationship in your life? Take the time now to ask for forgiveness. Even if you don't receive a response, know that it is a process specifically for your heart, and it is your release that is most important. God may work wonders in the meantime.

"In the end, we are our choices.
Build yourself a great story."
—Jeff Bezos, Amazon

Walk with Lori: Envision Leaping

Just a few questions for you as you begin to leap into purpose.

What is a dream you have that is so large it scares you? Can you place it in a dream bubble to manifest it?

What are your "and" opportunities in life? How will you extinguish the either/or choices and embrace more of the ands?

Where will you forgive in order to release to receive? What will you let go of? What will you keep?

chapter seven
Closing

There is a small town in southern Arizona, Bisbee. It was a copper mining town in the eighteen hundreds. It was even called the Queen of the Copper Camps. In the heights of its glory, it had exclusive hotels, restaurants, and saloons. It was carved out on the sides of the mountains and hills in the area. Driving into Bisbee, you wouldn't believe that over the mountain was this quaint community.

There is a wonderful little bed and breakfast there that I stayed in while working in the area a few years ago. I stayed over a weekend and had a chance to walk around the town and sample the charm of the small shops, markets, and historical sights. At one point I walked past a little steep set of stairs snuggled between a few homes that took you back to those times. A tiny, brass plaque commemorated the time in history that these almost forgotten steps were a reminder of. These were a set of 100-200 steps that took you from a lower side of the town to the upper side of the town. I walked those steps, straight up, realizing how far they went and how tiny they were. I wondered if I would make it all the way up. Do you know how I made it? You know the answer now: one step at a time! Just the way so many others had done in boots, petticoats, long dusters, and more. As I looked back down the entire view of where I had walked, I envisioned how our life was to be lived…just one step at a time.

How did Cary and Mark survive the challenges of Season 2 with attacks from cast members and many of the fans? One step at a time. How did Stephanie heal her heart and her friendship with Brandi Redmond even though she wondered when she started the journey if it would end in a friendship again? One step at a time. What's my number one recommendation when I work with clients? Take your journey one step at a time. Honor each step, and most of all…just get going. I'm blessed to travel each of these journeys, and it makes me remember to embrace each step of my own. I hope you will do the same.

What's Next?

How will you begin to step differently in your life? You may choose to walk a new path as you ignite intention even further. Each step will require your persistence, focus, and endurance. Who is going with you? Who will you need in your journey? What bridge will you encounter?

Continue to expand your new I AM's. Yes, sometimes you will experience endings that may create confusion, distress, and fear. They will lead you to a new I AM where you will find growth and a new journey awaiting you. It may even produce chaos. Wrap your arms around it, and focus and clarity will occur. You will be blessed in each step you take.

One of my favorite songs that helped me through many challenges in life was in the movie *The Preacher's Wife*, called "Step by Step." I wanted to share a piece of the lyrics with you as a reminder to just cross over the bridge and know you can take one step at a time to reach your dreams and the purpose for your life.

Well there's a bridge and there's a river that I still must cross
As I'm going on my journey
Oh, I might be lost
And there's a road I have to follow, a place I have to go
Well no-one told me just how to get there
But when I get there I'll know
Step By Step, Bit by Bit,
Stone By Stone, Brick by Brick
Step By Step, Day By Day, Mile by mile
And this old road is rough and ruined
So many dangers along the way
So many burdens might fall upon me
So many troubles that I have to face
Oh, but I won't let my spirit fail me
Oh, I won't let my spirit go
Until I get to my destination
I'm gonna take it slowly cause I'm making it mine.

Songwriter: Zemroy Thomas
"Step by Step" lyrics © Universal Music Publishing Group

As you find your own steps in the journey...remember to include:

Envision...

Release...

Manifest...

Gratitude...

Forgiveness...

If you ever want someone to walk a while with you as you step OUT, step UP, and step FORWARD in life, make sure you reach out to us.

Thank you for reading this book and I hope the stories, strategies, and insights will support you along your way in life and work.

ACKNOWLEDGMENTS

Thank you to our children, their loving spouses,
and our fabulous grandchildren, I love you all dearly.

Thank you dearly to my supportive editors...
I could not have done this without you!
Sarah Jones
Marvia Davidson
Katrina Kuzniuk

*Thank you to my "housewives" for letting me
share your lives with others...*
Stephanie Hollman and Cary Deuber

To my brilliant creative team...
Trey Stewart: for my photographs,
gorgeous cover, events, and social media
Karis Renee: for my website and book launch
Hair Styling by London Howell
Makeup design by Daniella Bell

Thank you to my precious...
Friends, clients, and colleagues who have willingly shared their stories

Looking for a dynamic speaker for your next event, retreat, conference, or women's program?

Lori would love to share her journey of insights, strategies, and stories from her best-selling book, *Step OUT, Step UP, Step Forward: How to Walk in Your Purpose.*

LORI L. DIXON, ED.S., is the owner of Walk with Lori, LLD Legacy and its affiliates, and LLD Legacy Publishing. Lori brings 35 years of knowledge working in education, business, healthcare, and nonprofits. As a spiritual visionary, therapist, author, speaker, and TV personality, she empowers others to re-envision their authentic self, activate their strengths, and embrace their journey in life. Lori strives to create approaches that support the ongoing shifts in life's most turbulent and challenging transitions. She is passionate about assisting others in their own transformational journey. With her dynamic television appearance on *The Real Housewives of Dallas*, Lori understands todays "reality" and how the ending to any story can be re-written. She believes in finding "the heart strings" in life, releasing the anchors of fears that hold one back and living the life we are meant to live and puts that into practice with her clients. She offers services through one on one sessions, small groups, workshops, retreats, and online programs. Lori's greatest blessings are her children, grandchildren, rescue kitties, and her amazing "co-pilot," her husband Art. Connect with Lori at WalkWithLori.com and on social media. For more information or to book Lori, email info@walkwithlori.com.

MEET THE EDITORS AND CREATIVE TEAM

Sarah Jones, Primary Editor, resides in Euless, TX, and is a mother to four beautiful children. She is currently living out her passion for communicating effectively through the written word, working as a freelance writer and editor for a magazine, websites, books and Bible studies. Sarah has over ten years of experiencing serving and teaching in ministry, primarily with children and teens. She aspires to move forward in spreading her message of hope, freedom and identity as a national author and speaker. Sarah values being intentional about living life on purpose. The following quote is instrumental in her process of living out this value: "My mission in life is not merely to survive, but to thrive; and to do so with some passion, some compassion, some humor, and some style." —Maya Angelou

Marvia Davidson, Secondary Editor and Creative Contributor, is a Texas writer/creative soul who enjoys writing, making art, laughing loudly, baking, dancing ridiculously because it's fun, and smashing lies that keep people from living whole. MarviaDavidson.com. You can also follow her: Twitter/Instagram @MarviaDavidson and Facebook at facebook.com/marviawrites.

Katrina Kuzniuk, Reviewing Editor, is an author, blogger, creative, and Reiki practitioner. Kat is committed to finding a voice for truths we are afraid to share, and bring them to life with understanding, and love. Born and raised in Canada, she resides in the United States with her beautiful family. She is looking forward to expanding her healing practice and explore opportunities for more writing adventures! info@KourageouslyKat.com

www.ingramcontent.com/pod-product-compliance
Lightning Source LLC
Chambersburg PA
CBHW020122130526
44591CB00032B/385